CHURCH IN SOCIETY

What people are saying about *Church in Society*:

Like a fine diamond, Don Hutchinson has highlighted the multifaceted responsibilities we carry as dual citizens, bringing heaven to earth for the benefit of others. Like a master jeweller, he has polished important gems of Scripture and society, giving clarity for the reader to better see the redemptive role of the Church in society. A must-read for those with interest in societal change.

—Barry Boucher
Founding Pastor, Lifecentre, Ottawa

Don Hutchinson has not only given Christians advice for public engagement but also how to practice a Christian life. Walk the walk and talk the talk!

—Janet Epp Buckingham
Director, Laurentian Leadership Centre,
Professor, Trinity Western University

Don Hutchinson is one of the most steadfast Christian leaders I know seeking to bridge the gap between people of faith and our nation's public square. His storytelling style and compelling illustrations give deep insights for anyone seeking to make a tangible difference in Canada today. Thank you, Don!

—Faytene Grasseschi
TV Host, Advocate, Author, Speaker

Don Hutchinson provides a sound rationale for the importance of Christian participation in helping shape a shared society focused on the common good. He extols Christian motivation, disapproves apathetic disinterest, and provides a practical guide for Christian engagement with public policy. A good read for those ready to reconsider the continuing value of the relationship between church and state.

—Willard Metzger
Executive Director, Citizens for Public Justice

Don Hutchinson draws on the wisdom and experience of first-century Christians to disciple twenty-first-century Christians into lives of personal significance that really matter. Hutchinson paints an attractive picture of a holistic and faithful Christian way of life.

—John Pellowe
CEO, Canadian Council of Christian Charities

Don Hutchinson is a tactical storyteller and *Church in Society* combines an interesting mix of biblical stories, tidbits from Canadian history, and autobiographical insights into a reflection on understanding citizenship as solidarity with our neighbours. The mix of personal and professional keeps the pace moving and challenges the reader to get beyond the easy answers into more nuanced challenges that face Canadian Christians in our twenty-first-century context.

—Ray Pennings
Executive Vice-President and Co-Founder, Cardus

Church in Society convinces Christian readers that our rights and responsibilities as citizens need to be *shalom*-based as we seek to be salt and light in a society that no longer presumes the public benefit of religious advancement. Don Hutchinson recounts life experiences, convicting his readers to remember our first responsibility mandated in Genesis—to be stewards of all that we have been given. He masterfully challenges twenty-first-century readers to reflect on first-century insight. Don's research is credibly engaging, as is his passion for the contribution that Christian faith brings to a nation. *Church in Society* is a refreshing and inspiring read, compelling both believers and non-believers to value religious rights. Don's discerning message is a timely voice to both church and society.

—Mary-Elsie Wolfe
Author, Pastor, Speaker

CHURCH IN SOCIETY

FIRST-CENTURY CITIZENSHIP LESSONS FOR
TWENTY-FIRST-CENTURY CHRISTIANS

DON HUTCHINSON

CHURCH IN SOCIETY
Copyright © 2019 by Don Hutchinson

Back cover author photo:
PMO Photo by Jason Ransom
www.jasonransom.com

All rights reserved. Neither this publication nor any part of this publication may be reproduced or transmitted in any form or by any means, electronic or mechanical, including photocopying, recording or any information storage and retrieval system, without permission in writing from the author.

Unless otherwise indicated, all Scripture quotations are from the ESV® Bible (The Holy Bible, English Standard Version®), copyright © 2001 by Crossway, a publishing ministry of Good News Publishers. Used by permission. All rights reserved. Scripture quotations marked (KJV) are taken from the Holy Bible, King James Version, which is in the public domain. Scripture quotations taken from the Amplified® Bible (AMP), Copyright © 2015 by The Lockman Foundation. Used by permission. www.Lockman.org. Scripture taken from the New American Standard Bible ® (NASB) copyright © 1960, 1962, 1963, 1968, 1971, 1972, 1973, 1975, 1977, 1995 by The Lockman Foundation. Used by permission. www.Lockman.org. Scripture quotations marked (NIV) are taken from the Holy Bible, New International Version®, NIV®. Copyright © 1973, 1978, 1984, 2011 by Biblica, Inc.™ Used by permission of Zondervan. All rights reserved worldwide. www.zondervan.com The "NIV" and "New International Version" are trademarks registered in the United States Patent and Trademark Office by Biblica, Inc.™

Print ISBN: 978-1-4866-1930-6
eBook ISBN: 978-1-4866-1931-3

Word Alive Press
119 De Baets Street, Winnipeg, MB R2J 3R9
www.wordalivepress.ca

Cataloguing in Publication may be obtained through Library and Archives Canada

This book is dedicated to:

Gloria, Grace, and John
Thank you for daily helping to clarify for me what
it means to follow Jesus.

CONTENTS

Foreword — xiii
Acknowledgements — xv
Preface — xix
Introduction — xxvii

PART I: CHURCH

1. Saul of Tarsus, Model Citizen — 3
2. Paul of Tarsus, Citizen Model — 11
3. The Church, People of the Word — 19
4. The Church, Many Parts, One Body — 29
5. One Body, When One Part Suffers — 39
6. Christians, Dual Citizens in the World — 49

PART II: IN SOCIETY

7. The Church, Citizens in the Nation — 59
8. The State, Citizens' Rights and Religion — 69
9. The State, Government Benefits — 81
10. The Church, Lifestyle of Generosity — 91
11. The Church, Public Engagement — 101
12. The Church, Politics — 113
13. The Church, Media — 129
14. The Church, The Environment — 145

Conclusion
    Conclusion   159
    Epilogue, The Dual Citizens' Prayer   173

Appendix I: The Nicene Creed   175
Appendix II: The Apostles' Creed   177
Appendix III: *Christian Witness in a Multi-Religious World: Recommendations for Conduct*   179

Bibliography   187
About the Author   205

He has told you, O man, what is good; and what does the Lord require of you but to do justice, and to love kindness, and to walk humbly with your God?

—Micah 6:8

FOREWORD

Don Hutchinson in *Church in Society* weaves his way through biblical text, early church history, and personal travels and stories to help us see the power and beauty of the church, what we know as the "bride of Christ." He has purpose in connecting these strands: to point us in the direction of engaging as citizens, here and now.

Not unlike Augustine, Bishop of Hippo, in *City of God*, who called his first-century church to see the Spirit at work, this author in *Church in Society* reminds the twenty-first-century church that "heavenly citizenship informs our participation in earthly citizenship." This is of course difficult. But author Don Hutchinson presses us not to abandon our calling by opting for a one-dimensional view.

This message is both biblical and timely, a reminder that taking the easy way out has never been the biblical mandate.

—Brian C. Stiller
Global Ambassador, World Evangelical Alliance

ACKNOWLEDGEMENTS

The wind blows where it wishes, and you hear its sound, but you do not know where it comes from or where it goes. So it is with everyone who is born of the Spirit.

—John 3:8

Over the course of nearly six decades, I have made a lot of repeat trips on airplanes. As a child, summer after summer started with the flight from Toronto, Canada to San Juan, Puerto Rico, with the return flight in August. More recently, there have been multiple flights between Ottawa and Toronto. The airports might look familiar, but the choice of runway changes depending on the wind.

When Guillaume Duvieusart suggested I consider putting together a shorter book than *Under Siege: Religious Freedom and the Church in Canada at 150 (1867–2017)*[1] based on an adaptation of Part III of that book, I was reluctant. It felt like cheating for me to repackage a portion of my first book. Around the same time, Twitter started to fill with stories of Christian authors producing shorter, updated, or altered versions of previously published works. Some months later, after an evening of dinner and conversation with friends, I agreed to take on the project.

The airport might look familiar, but the choice of runway is determined by the wind. And the wind blows where it wishes. Thank you, Guillaume, for hearing the Voice in the wind and suggesting this book.

---

1   Don Hutchinson, *Under Siege: Religious Freedom and the Church in Canada at 150 (1867–2017)* (Winnipeg, MB: Word Alive Press, 2017).

What might have seemed a relatively simple task followed the wind to what you now hold in your hands. It represents more than a repackaging of that Part III. *Church in Society* took off based on that text, but as the wind blew it has landed on a different runway.

Although not quoted in this book, foundational to my understanding of Christian citizenship are two books by Brian Stiller, one of the deans of contemporary Christian involvement in the Canadian public square:[2] *From the Tower of Babel to Parliament Hill: How to Be a Christian in Canada Today*[3] and *Jesus and Caesar: Christians in the Public Square*.[4] Both of these are among the fruit of Brian's time as president of The Evangelical Fellowship of Canada. Among his more recent writing, contributing to the formation of my thought patterns on the global Church, are *An Insider's Guide to Praying for the World*[5] and *From Jerusalem to Timbuktu: A World Tour of the Spread of Christianity*,[6] fruit of his service as global ambassador for the World Evangelical Alliance. I am honoured to have Brian provide the foreword for *Church in Society*.

Constructive feedback received from Janet Epp-Buckingham, John Pellowe, Mary-Elsie Wolfe, and the reviewers for the Word Alive Press Free Publishing Contest proved valuable in improving the content you have in your hands, addressing oversights in the original manuscript.

Much appreciation *part deux* to the team at Word Alive Press. As the saying goes, we got the band back together. Tia Friesen (née Scarborough) again shepherded the book through the process from manuscript to publication as project manager. It was Tia who alerted me to the Word Alive Press Free Publishing Contest, in which the manuscript for *Church in Society* found a place on the 2019 non-fiction shortlist. Evan Braun edits in a way that makes my writing better, and more readable. Nikki has

---

2   For a summary of these Canadians, see: Hutchinson, *Under Siege*, 180–186.
3   Brian C. Stiller, *From the Tower of Babel to Parliament Hill: How to Be a Christian in Canada Today* (Toronto, ON: HarperCollins Publishers Ltd., 1997).
4   Brian C. Stiller, *Jesus and Caesar: Christians in the Public Square* (Oakville, ON: Castle Quay Books Canada, 2003).
5   Brian C. Stiller, *An Insider's Guide to Praying for the World* (Grand Rapids, MI: Bethany House, 2016).
6   Brian C. Stiller, *From Jerusalem to Timbuktu: A World Tour of the Spread of Christianity* (Downers Grove, IL: InterVarsity Press, 2018).

designed another great cover, complementary to *Under Siege*, and Konrad has done the same with layout. Thank you.

Errors are mine alone.

Special thanks to the Thursday morning breakfast group—pastors, authors, and leaders who weekly proffer solutions to problems of Church, world, and professional sports teams, and most importantly support one another in the reality of holding on as best we can to the hem of His garment while encouraging others to strengthen their grip.

Soli Deo gloria.

PREFACE

Only let your manner of life be worthy [alt. Only behave as citizens worthy] of the gospel of Christ, so that whether I come and see you or am absent, I may hear of you that you are standing firm in one spirit, with one mind striving side by side for the faith of the gospel, and not frightened in anything by your opponents.

—Philippians 1:27–28

"When Christ calls a man, he bids him come and die"[7] are the first words one sees when beginning to read Dietrich Bonhoeffer's *The Cost of Discipleship*. I dare add, when Christ calls a man He also bids him come and live, just as a woman called by Christ is bidden to die to self, as well as to then live for Christ. Jesus said that He came so that we might have a more abundant life (John 10:10). Our life is lived in community, in community with others who are following Christ as well as those who are not. That abundant life takes place through us, as citizens, where we live.

Citizenship, the topic of this book, is about more than voting and governmental politics. Citizenship refers to our life together as neighbours; as residents on the same street, in the same city, in the same nation, on the same planet. Christian citizenship also includes the influences and responsibilities that come with the promise of heaven, and with earthly Christ-following.

---

7   Dietrich Bonhoeffer, *The Cost of Discipleship* (London, UK: SCM Press Ltd., 1949), 7.

Yes, Christ calls us first to die, to die daily to self (Matthew 16:24; Mark 8:34; Luke 9:23), and then to live, to live for Him (Galatians 2:20), sharing His interest in all of humanity and all of creation.

In the pages ahead, I hope to both inform and challenge your perspective on citizenship as a Christian. Like much of twenty-first-century Christianity, you and I have been influenced by the changing society in which we live. What if we could reverse that influence so that instead of changes in society influencing us, as Christians you and I influenced the changes in society?

The first-century writers of the New Testament reveal a Christianity that adapted within its culture—even today, we Christians look like those around us. The early Christians lived a lifestyle that influenced changes in their society until over time the cultural shape of the Western world was referred to as having a Judeo-Christian heritage.

What if instead of nostalgically looking back, like the Israelites on their journey from Egypt longing for a time that perhaps never really was, we deliberately chose to learn the lessons chronicled by Christian citizens of the first century and look forward? This book is about looking forward to a future neighbourhood, city, nation, and world influenced by the way we live our lives, person by person, Christian by Christian, congregation by congregation, denomination by denomination, as the Church in society.

Citizenship is about more than politics, and Christian citizenship is about even more.

I'm a storyteller, so I will share in a storytelling style, beginning each chapter with applicable Scripture from His story. This book will tell stories from the first-century and twenty-first-century Church, and I'll include a bit of my own story as a Christian Canadian to provide context on my perspective. Throughout, I'll share thoughts on how we might effectively live our Christianity in the nation where we dwell, citizens of both heaven and earth.

A friend once told me, "All theology is experiential." By that, he was saying that our understanding of God and Christian life are shaped by our experiences. Experiences with the people we know. Experiences from our involvement in the life of the congregation we attend and in which we worship. The influence of books and other things we read. Particularities of the nation in which we live, etc.

This book is informed, and necessarily limited, by my experiences. Hopefully, it will contribute to your practical theology of living life as a Christian and a citizen where you are.

Don't be afraid of the word *theology*. It's simply a term to describe a process all Christians journey through as we think about who God is, what we believe about God, and how our lives intersect and interact with God. And if our theology is not *practical*, what is it? Our theology is to be practiced in all of life, not just in religious exercises. Our theology is to have influence in every aspect of our lives, as well as influencing the lives our lives touch.

This is not a new idea. It was part of the framework for the theology of John Wesley, who coined the term *practical divinity* to "describe his understanding of the nature and purpose of theology."[8] For Wesley, theological reflection consistently posed a challenge to assess Christianity's outworking in practical service. Wesley was neither the first nor the last to reach that conclusion.

Because I'm a storyteller, let me begin with a short story, a true story that became an inspiration for the title of this book, *Church in Society*.

Canada wasn't supposed to host the 1967 World Expo. But in 1962, the Soviet Union backed out of its commitment to hold Expo '67 in Moscow, originally intended to celebrate the fiftieth anniversary of the Russian Revolution. Aggressive pursuit of the unexpected opportunity presented by the 1962 Soviet decision resulted in approval from the Bureau International des Expositions to invite the world to Montreal, Quebec, as part of Canada's centennial celebrations.[9]

It was likely unanticipated that the Expo '67 theme, Man and His World, would be anything more than an invitation for nations to display

---

8   Thomas A. Langford, *Practical Divinity: Theology for the Wesleyan Tradition* (Nashville, TN: Abingdon Press, 1983), Preface.
9   "Expo 67," J.H. Marsh, ed., *The Canadian Encyclopedia, Second Edition* (Edmonton, AB: Hurtig Publishers, 1988), Volume II, 738; and S. Banerjee, "Fifty Years Later, Montreal's Iconic Expo 67 Still Resonates," *Toronto Star*. April 26, 2017 (https://www.thestar.com/news/canada/2017/04/26/fifty-years-later-montreals-iconic-expo-67-still-resonates.html).

their accomplishments. But the anthropocentric focus was also a marker of change in disposition for Canadian, North American, and the Western culture which was transitioning from Christendom—centred in Judeo-Christian foundations, and governance heavily influenced by the Church—to secular pluralism.

Expo '67 itself was a wonder of human accomplishment. The location required enlarging an existing island in the St. Lawrence River, and even building a new one!

Man and His World was divided into five subthemes: Man the Creator, Man the Explorer, Man the Producer, Man the Provider, and Man and the Community. In addition to sixty nation pavilions, there were fifty-three private pavilions and thousands of private exhibitors spread throughout the site.

More than fifty million people attended Canada's International and Universal Exposition (the official name) and the decision was made to maintain a permanent exhibition on the Expo site. It would take on the Expo theme name as its own, Man and His World. Most nations were delighted to donate their pavilions to the venture, saving the cost of tearing them down. Montreal's Man and His World would stay open until 1981.[10]

The theme that carried forward impacted the secondary school curriculum which taught Canadian civics. In my high school, the civics course was called "Man in Society." In addition to the basics of municipal, provincial, and federal political structures, voting, and other aspects of political participation, we were introduced to the significant contributions of humankind through civic government, from public education to infrastructure construction and space exploration. In short, an anthropocentric world was described as a world of endless opportunity, and a world destined to a peaceful existence through democratic governance.

We bought it. At least, most did. We believed Canada was the world leader in peacekeeping, and we believed our democratic form of government enabled and encouraged our participation in a world inevitably headed toward a peaceful future.

---

10 "Expo 67 Man and His World," *Library and Archives Canada*. Date of access: August 12, 2018 (https://www.collectionscanada.gc.ca/expo/0533020602_e.html).

PREFACE

The original *Star Trek*[11] television series had aired around the same time as marketing for Expo '67 started. A decade later, *Star Trek* reruns were the most popular show among me and my classmates. Between Man in Society and the United Federation of Planets'[12] form of government expressed in *Star Trek*, we tacitly accepted that the United Nations would bring peace on Earth, goodwill to mankind.

Missing from this context was the foundational reason for living life together. The motivation to explore, whether on Earth or in space ("where no man has gone before"[13]), was curiosity. For athletes, the motivation for sports was victory and reward; for spectators, entertainment. What was the motivation for desiring the common good, human flourishing? Was it just a product of evolution? Was humankind simply being driven genetically toward getting along? Or was there something more?

The neighbourhood where I grew up was diverse. My parents and older sisters had come from Barbados. Neighbours were multigenerational Canadians, as well as immigrants from Poland, Germany, England, India, Pakistan, South Africa, and the United States, among others. Protestants lived side by side with Catholics, non-churchgoers, and people from religions about which I knew little. Mostly white-skinned, we were well-seasoned with a peppering of black and brown. The boys gathered around hockey, football, baseball, and sledding, and, as we matured, music and girls. We got along. We cared for each other. This was our

---

11 American screenwriter and producer Gene Roddenberry created *Star Trek* as a kind of science fiction soap-opera spaghetti-western in space. *Star Trek* made its television debut in 1966. The *USS Enterprise*, on which most of the action took place, was one starship in the Starfleet of the United Federation of Planets.
12 *Star Trek*'s United Federation of Planets, established in the twenty-second century, was based on a utopian interplanetary version of the United Nations. Member planets retained their political and societal structures. For purposes of advancing peace, providing defence, and engaging in space exploration, and based on principles of liberty, universal rights for sentient/intelligent lifeforms, and equality among those species, they voluntarily participated under the central authority of the Federation.
13 From the *Star Trek* original series' opening title sequence catchphrase: "Space: the final frontier. These are the voyages of the starship Enterprise. Its five-year mission: to explore strange new worlds, to seek out new life and new civilizations, to boldly go where no man has gone before!" Later adaptations changed the final phrase to the gender-neutral "to boldly go where no one has gone before!"

Canada. For many of us, this was our experience of what the world was like—or at least, what we thought the world was supposed to be like.

We didn't have the internet. There was no social media. News cycles were filtered through print (daily), radio (hourly summaries), and television (reports at 6:00 p.m. and 11:00 p.m.). In the Toronto area, we could pick up fewer than a dozen TV stations (two dozen after cable), AM and FM radio, and three daily newspapers (*The Telegram*, *The Globe and Mail*, and the *Toronto Daily Star*). Reports about confrontation, conflict, or combat were rare, and the location of such things was, to us, distant.

Those who have read *Under Siege*[14] will know I didn't become a Christian until just before the Christmas after my twenty-first birthday.[15] I'm not sure whether it was because of my assumption that all Canadians were Christians—living as we did in a Christian nation, as it were—or my personal inattention to anything religious, or the possibility that my Christian neighbours might have been observant of *Star Trek*'s Prime Directive, but I don't recall much talk about religion or church apart from who went to public school and who went to Catholic school.

Starfleet General Order 1, the Prime Directive, was the guiding principle of space exploration for the United Federation of Planets. In the *Star Trek* episode "Bread and Circuses," a story about a planet with a twentieth-century version of the Roman Empire where the landing crew from the *USS Enterprise* were captured by a group of runaway slaves from a persecuted minority religious group called Children of the Son, the Prime Directive was summarized in a conversation between Captain James Tiberius Kirk, First Officer Spock, and Chief Medical Officer Dr. Leonard McCoy.

> SPOCK: Then the Prime Directive is in full force, Captain?
> KIRK: No identification of self or mission. No interference with the social development of said planet.

---

14 Hutchinson, *Under Siege*, xxi.
15 If you missed that earlier volume, I will cover the story briefly in the upcoming Introduction.

> MCCOY: No references to space, or the fact that there are other worlds or more advanced civilizations.[16]

Many Christians live as if *Star Trek*'s Prime Directive applies on Earth as it does in Gene Rodenberry's fictional heavens. We are cautious to ensure there is no identification of self or mission, or any interference with the social development of others. We make no reference to that which is not immediately observable or the fact that there is more to life than this temporal world, the truth that another civilization is present and awaits just beyond the reach of what our eyes can see.

In a nation where secularism is advancing, observable and theoretical science aspire to define the parameters of belief. Atheism is reinforced by scientific methodologists and enforced by ardent activist non-believers. It is preferred by those who consider heaven to be fictional that religious belief be kept private, religious worship take place within the containment of a private building, and religious practices not infringe on the public sphere.

However, as I wrote in *Under Siege*,

> Christian faith is personal, intimately personal. And Christianity was always intended to be public, engaging, and sincere in its expression—not just private. Being a Christ-follower is a both/and experience, not an either/or one. We need to have the private devotion to follow and the public expression to convict us if we are ever on trial for being Christian.[17]

What that public expression looks like may be different for each Christian, set in the interactive context of personal capacity, personal commitment, and local laws, but there will be public expression of some sort if we are more than just converts to Christianity, if we are in fact *disciples* of Jesus Christ.

---

16 *Star Trek*, "Bread and Circuses." Season 2, Episode 25. Directed by Ralph Senensky. Written by Gene Roddenberry & Gene L. Coon. NBC, March 15, 1968.
17 Hutchinson, *Under Siege*, 249.

It was Jesus who summarized the two great commandments from the Old Testament and gave us a third, His new commandment for those who follow Him:

1. Love the Lord our God (Mark 12:30).
2. Love our neighbours as ourselves (Mark 12:31).
3. Love one another—by this, the world will know we are His disciples (John 13:34–35).

Loving God will usher us into relationships beyond ourselves.

First, we will enter into relationship with other disciples, the Church; then, with our neighbours (society), including those neighbours who do not share our faith.

Exploring the relationships that arise from loving God—because we have a deep-seated desire to know God and His plan for our lives—is key to what this book is about. It also provides vital insight into the motivation, the foundational reason, for living life together. Life is not just about *man* in society; it's about you and me and the community of people who are in relationship with God and one another, i.e. the Church, living with and influencing others in a shared society. Church in society.

Three Takeaways

- Citizenship is about more than voting and politics. Citizenship is about living life together.
- Christians' Christianity has been influenced by society.
- Christian faith is personal and intended to be shared, not just private.

INTRODUCTION

Not that I have already obtained this or am already perfect, but I press on to make it my own, because Christ Jesus has made me his own. Brothers, I do not consider that I have made it my own. But one thing I do: forgetting what lies behind and straining forward to what lies ahead, I press on toward the goal for the prize of the upward call of God in Christ Jesus.

—Philippians 3:12–14

Christianity is not a Western religion, although it has been the dominant religion in Western society for centuries, shaping the culture, and being shaped by the culture as well.

Jesus was born in the Middle East, in Bethlehem; raised in the Middle East, in Nazareth; and nurtured in an ancient Middle Eastern religion, Judaism. Jesus' birth family and heritage was indigenous to Israel. Jesus was not Roman, i.e. he was not a Westerner. Christianity, referred to early on as *"the Way"* (John 14:6; Act 9:2; 19:9, 23), was birthed as a fulfillment of the prophecies found in the sacred texts of Judaism.

Christianity is a contextual religion. Its foundational truth that Jesus is the Christ (in Hebrew, *Messiah*, and in literal translation to English, *Anointed One*) fits within any culture. The contextual nature of Christianity was confirmed by the Christian council at Jerusalem when they welcomed converts from the culturally dissimilar Greeks and Romans (from the West) without requiring them to become Jewish (a Middle Eastern religion) in order to be Christ-followers (Acts 15:6–29). The disciples were first called Christians at Antioch, in Syria, in the Middle East (Acts 11:26). Christians, meaning "little anointed ones," became the descriptor of Christ's followers that took hold—and it remains to this day.

Context is important. The Church may look different *in* different contexts and *from* different contexts. That's because people interact with the context in which they find themselves. It's vital to be aware that context—life experience, law, and culture—is constantly changing, whether slowly or more rapidly. The Church, composed of people, is interactive in the context of the community, city, country, time period, etc. in which Christians live.

Sometimes we make the mistake, based on our necessarily limited personal experiences, of thinking that other people are like us. That their experiences are like ours. That they think like us. That they act like us. Even that they will like us. We also make the corollary mistake of thinking people who are not like us will not like us.

Context is important. Understanding the context of the other may be important for our getting along with one another. And remember, the context of our own experiences shapes our practical theology, including how we live out the *love your neighbour* commandment.

Before considering the Church and its interaction with society, here is some background information about the author that provides context for my thoughts about the Church in society.

While I was in high school, George Lucas prompted a generation planet-wide to take religion out of the private sphere and into the public sphere with the release of the first *Star Wars* movie. *Star Wars* introduced us to Jedi knights, dressed like holy men of old, training disciples who sensed and interacted with the Force.[18]

Even for a non-religious guy like me, *Star Wars* was transparently a religious movie. It was also a space western, and I liked westerns. The light side and the dark side were expressions of the classic white hats and black hats, good and evil. Luke Skywalker dressed in white, Darth Vader in black. Obi-Wan Kenobi wore a simple religious robe over white clothing. Anyone familiar with Friar Tuck from Robin Hood's Sherwood

---

18 *Star Wars*, directed by George Lucas (Los Angeles, CA: Twentieth Century Fox, 1977).

Forest knew Kenobi was a religious guy just by seeing the brown-hooded robe. And Skywalker was his apprentice, in quest of his own robe.

In May 1977, I was supposed to be preparing to write Grade Twelve final exams. The metaphysical powers of the Force were far more interesting than anything I should have been studying.

There was no clear explanation as to why some people were better attuned to the Force. *Star Wars* was just a movie. But it seemed we all wanted the Force to be with us. "May the Force be with you" had a ring of genuine encouragement about it.[19] I watched the movie several times and didn't study as much as I might have.

A little before George Lucas introduced us to the fictional Force, I had an experience that got me thinking about the non-fictional God. I had an unexpected personal prompting that *God* wanted *me* in His ministry. No specifics, just the idea of God, a sense that God was still engaged with humanity and somehow wanted me to serve others on His behalf. I didn't know how or who or what or where or why, but the when of the prompting was *now*. I had lots of questions about that prompting, questions which had gone largely unanswered in my exploration from an unchurched background.

And then the Force came along. Religion in the open, if only in a movie, gave me the impetus to continue my search for answers.

I'd thought I was a Christian because I equated being Christian with being Canadian, but I didn't really know what a Christian was.

A friend invited me to an event in the gymnasium at our high school that featured professional athletes who shared about the importance of having Jesus *in your life*. Afterward, the athletes stuck around to sign autographs and chat. I had gone for the sports heroes, but in the process I encountered the event's staff sponsor—the school's incessantly smiley librarian—along with other staff and students I hadn't known were Christians but knew from class and a variety of extracurricular activities.

When I arrived at Queen's University, where I studied history and politics, I came across a number of students who I had met for the first

---

19 It would be more than two decades before *Star Wars, Episode I: The Phantom Menace* would offer an explanation about midichlorians, microscopic creatures whose measurable presence determined sensitivity to the Force.

time in that gym. I attended a few Queen's Christian Fellowship events, and in my second year I hosted a Bible study group in my dormitory room.[20] One of the young women from the gym experience led the study and we read through the Gospel of Mark. Every week I borrowed a Bible.

That Christmas, my Aunt Barbara and Uncle Joe visited Toronto from Texas. My gift from them was a large, heavy, leather-bound Bible with the words of Jesus printed in red, an array of study features, and my name engraved in gold lettering on the front. I was seriously prepared to stop borrowing a Bible when I went back to school!

Owning the biggest and best Bible didn't make me a Christian, though. Somehow I had missed the plot in Mark, although I determined to plough through the rest of the Bible.

At spring convocation in 1981, I graduated with my Bachelor of Arts, was headed to law school, and planned for a career in politics. While at Queen's, I read a fair bit of the Bible, took a world religions course (for which I wrote a paper on the historic Jesus; there's a lot of historic material that confirms the life and death of Jesus from Nazareth, as well as claims of His resurrection), and was still clueless about the whole being a Christian thing.

That August, a young woman invited me to her church. She attended The Salvation Army. A few weeks later, I moved to Vancouver to attend law school at the University of British Columbia. In my mind, if she and I were going to stay in touch I needed to find and attend a Salvation Army church. The Kitsilano Corps was a short bicycle ride from where I lived.

As noted in *Under Siege*,

> Not being wise to the ways of the Church, and too proud to say I didn't know better, when I saw the push-in-the-plastic-letters notice board that said services were on Sundays at 11:00 a.m. and 6:30 p.m. and Bible study on Wednesdays at 7:00 p.m., I assumed going to church meant attending all three. So I did.[21]

---

20 Before each Bible study, I would push my girlfriend's stuff under the bed; she wasn't interested in my Christian friends, so she always left before the group arrived.
21 Hutchinson, *Under Siege*, xx.

INTRODUCTION

It took me until November to realize I wasn't actually a Christian, despite having read the Bible from cover to cover by that time and having a near perfect attendance record at church, three times a week.

I spent Saturday, December 5, 1981 reading German pastor and theologian Dietrich Bonhoeffer's book *The Cost of Discipleship*. I was captured from the opening words of the foreword by Anglican Bishop George Bell:

> "When Christ calls a man," says Dietrich Bonhoeffer, "he bids him come and die."[22]

I was convicted by the time I reached its closing words:

> The disciple looks solely at his Master. But when a man follows Jesus Christ and bears the image of the incarnate, crucified and risen Lord, when he has become the image of God, we may at last say that he has been called to be the "imitator of God." The follower of Jesus is the imitator of God. "Be ye there for imitators of God, as beloved children" (Ephesians 5:1).[23]

At around 10:30 p.m., I made the decision to become a disciple—an imitator—of Jesus Christ and make it public by going forward to kneel at the mercy seat (the prayer bench at the front of Salvation Army worship halls) the next morning at church.

At the conclusion of first year law studies, I left school to prepare for ministry as an officer (pastor) in The Salvation Army. A few years after becoming a pastor, I was asked by the leader of The Salvation Army in Canada to return to law school, complete my law degree, and establish a national legal department.

Although my time in leadership with The Salvation Army ended just before the turn of the century, I was introduced through it to the unique legal challenges and commitments of living out Christian faith in Canada and North America. Subsequently, I was privileged to work

---

22 Dietrich Bonhoeffer, *The Cost of Discipleship* (London, UK: SCM Press Ltd., 1949), 7.
23 Ibid., 344.

with national and international ministries where my eyes were opened more fully to the global Church (the Body of Christ) and the diverse challenges—legal, social, political, and religious/ideological—faced by Christians in different parts of the world.

As a lawyer, I encountered principles of religious freedom, belief, and practice in the context of law. As a Christian, I encountered principles of religious freedom and Christian living in the context of Scripture and the contemporary Church, both local and global. They are principles we as Christ-followers are bidden to practice in the context of our daily lives as citizens.

Together, in the following pages, let's consider our place in the context of the Church, our place with the Church in the context of society, and the application of citizenship principles which reveal that our lives belong to Christ.

Three Takeaways

- Christianity is not a Western religion, but a contextual religion.
- We make the mistakes of thinking people are like us, and those who are not like us won't like us.
- The Church functions in the context of the society in which Christians live.

PART I:
CHURCH

When he had washed their feet and put on his outer garments and resumed his place, he said to them, "Do you understand what I have done to you? You call me Teacher and Lord, and you are right, for so I am. If I then, your Lord and Teacher, have washed your feet, you also ought to wash one another's feet. For I have given you an example, that you also should do just as I have done to you."

—John 13:12–15

A new commandment I give to you, that you love one another: just as I have loved you, you also are to love one another. By this all people will know that you are my disciples, if you have love for one another.

—John 13:34–35

For as in one body we have many members, and the members do not all have the same function, so we, though many, are one body in Christ, and individually members one of another. Having gifts that differ according to the grace given to us, let us use them: if prophecy, in proportion to our faith; if service, in our serving; the one who teaches, in his teaching; the one who exhorts, in his exhortation; the one who contributes, in generosity; the one who leads, with zeal; the one who does acts of mercy, with cheerfulness.

Let love be genuine. Abhor what is evil; hold fast to what is good. Love one another with brotherly affection. Outdo one another in showing honor. Do not be slothful in zeal, be fervent in spirit, serve the Lord. Rejoice in hope, be patient in tribulation, be constant in prayer. Contribute to the needs of the saints and seek to show hospitality.

—Romans 12:4–13

CHAPTER ONE

SAUL OF TARSUS, MODEL CITIZEN

> *I am a Jew, born in Tarsus in Cilicia, but brought up in this city, educated at the feet of Gamaliel according to the strict manner of the law of our fathers, being zealous for God as all of you are this day. I persecuted this Way to the death, binding and delivering to prison both men and women, as the high priest and the whole council of elders can bear me witness. From them I received letters to the brothers, and I journeyed toward Damascus to take those also who were there and bring them in bonds to Jerusalem to be punished.*
>
> —Acts 22:3–5

IF, AS I SOMETIMES DO, YOU SKIPPED THE PREFACE AND INTRODUCTION TO HEAD straight to the first chapter, kind of like skipping soup and salad to get to the meat and potatoes, let me catch you up before you start reading.[24]

At one time or another, you've likely thought about how a relatively small group from an outcast religion affected the world to the point where two millennia later much of the planet is considered either to have a Christian heritage or to have been influenced in societal formation by the presence of Christians. You have likely also contemplated how that heritage has been eroded, even during your lifetime. This book will explore written guidance provided by those first-century world-shapers who were first called Christians at Antioch (Acts 11:26), guidance that imparts the foundations for how they influenced change in the world and how you and I can contribute to it happening again.

---

24 By the way, the soup and salad are a chosen complement to the meal.

PART I: CHURCH

As Christians, we have been influenced by changes in the society in which we live. This book presents thoughts on how we in turn can influence the neighbourhoods, cities, nations, and even the world in which we are citizens for the purpose of shaping emerging and future societal patterns.

Key to those thoughts, we'll learn from the stories and instruction of the first-century contributors to the New Testament, with each chapter being introduced by relevant Scripture. Through the telling of stories, you'll get the benefit of thought-provoking experiences, truth, and strategies to influence the world in which you live for its betterment, and for Christ.

Let's start by looking at a readily recognizable story.

Christmas this year will be celebrated in pretty much the same way it has been for decades, even centuries, depending on where you live and how you celebrate. In some households, it is a different celebration from what it once was. My childhood celebrations were focused on Santa Claus, gifts, and family. The message conveyed by Linus about the true meaning of Christmas in my favourite seasonal television special, *A Charlie Brown Christmas*,[25] gave me more a sense of warm comfort than an acceptable explanation of truth.

But one December day in 1981, that changed. When I accepted the truth of what Linus shared, the focus of my Christmas celebrations became the advent and birth of Jesus of Nazareth, called Christ.[26]

The neighbourhood in which I grew up featured a variety of Christmas traditions. There were those, like us, who celebrated Santa Claus and family without questioning the true meaning of Christmas.

---

25 *A Charlie Brown Christmas*, directed by Bill Melendez (Los Angeles, CA: CBS, 1965).
26 Much of the New Testament was written to a Greek-speaking non-Jewish (Gentile) audience of Christ-followers, and to Hellenistic (Greek-speaking) Jewish followers of Jesus. As a result, the expected Messiah of the Old Testament is referred to as Christ in the New Testament. *Messiah* is the English transliteration (written pronunciation) of the Hebrew/Aramaic. *Christ* is similarly the English transliteration of the Greek for the same word. The English translation of the word used in both languages is *Anointed One*, a reference to the One chosen by God. (For more information, see footnote 36.)

There were neighbours who attended a birth of Christ mass or other forms of Christmas church service, either late on December 24 or on the morning of December 25, and others marked it two weeks later on January 6–7, dependant on whether their celebration was based on the Gregorian calendar (Western, i.e. Roman Catholic and Protestant) or the Julian calendar (Eastern, i.e. Orthodox). Consistent from one home to the next was a decorated tree in a main room of the house.

For a significant number in the Body of Christ around the world, Christmas celebrations are, for safety reasons, relatively private and quiet, even secret. In dozens of nations, Christians are persecuted for their beliefs, beliefs that run counter to those of either a religious or ideological majority who see the Church as a threat.

Some Christmas celebrations, and seasonal publications, entertain an annual deliberation about the actual birthdate of Jesus of Nazareth—who, history tells us, was born in Bethlehem. Like Linus, you and I can read the story in Luke 2.[27]

Is the precise date important? Queen Elizabeth II was born on April 21, 1926 but her official birthday celebration takes place with the annual military parade and celebration of the monarch's birthday on the second Saturday in June.[28] The nation celebrates in June even though the birth was on a different date.

There might be debate about the date of Jesus' birth, but few in the twenty-first century question the historicity of His birth.

---

27 This is what Christmas is all about, Charlie Brown: *"And there were in the same country shepherds abiding in the field, keeping watch over their flock by night. And, lo, the angel of the Lord came upon them, and the glory of the Lord shone round about them: and they were sore afraid. And the angel said unto them, Fear not: for, behold, I bring you good tidings of great joy, which shall be to all people. For unto you is born this day in the city of David a Saviour, which is Christ the Lord. And this shall be a sign unto you; ye shall find the babe wrapped in swaddling clothes, lying in a manger. And suddenly there was with the angel a multitude of the heavenly host praising God, and saying, Glory to God in the highest, and on earth peace, good will toward men"* (Luke 2:8–14, KJV).
28 Megan McCluskey, "Here's Why Queen Elizabeth II Has Two Birthdays." *TIME*, April 20, 2018 (http://time.com/5248082/queen-elizabeth-two-birthdays).

Other historical references in Luke's account have been borne out as accurate.[29] Non-Christ-following historians have also affirmed the life and crucifixion of Jesus, as well as the claims by His followers of a third-day resurrection from death to life.[30]

Was Jesus the long-awaited Jewish Messiah? Many believed Him to be so, and word of His resurrection spread quickly. Others did not. Efforts to silence the Christ-followers were harsh.

Whatever else has changed over the last two thousand years, human nature remains much the same. People have a tendency to pick a side on an issue and it's difficult to change their minds. Some people are willing to die for their beliefs. Others are prepared to kill for theirs.

Saul of Tarsus was one such person in the latter group, ready to kill to preserve the purity of his faith and the faith community to which he belonged.

Saul was born in the city of Tarsus, in the Roman province of Cilicia, modern-day Turkey. Tarsus was a Greek-speaking city. Given the name Saul, perhaps in recognition of Israel's first king, he described himself in letters written later in life as *"a Hebrew of Hebrews"* (Philippians 3:5). Greek would have been Saul's second language, used in Tarsus

---

29   Lee Strobel, *The Case for Christmas: A Journalist Investigates the Identity of the Child in the Manger* (Grand Rapids, MI: Zondervan, 2005), 42–45; and J. Warner Wallace, "A Brief Sample of Archaeology Corroborating the Claims of the New Testament," *Cold-Case Christianity*. June 8, 2018 (http://coldcasechristianity.com/2018/a-brief-sample-of-archaeology-corroborating-the-claims-of-the-new-testament).

30   Some of the earliest affirmations in non-Christian sources are from Flavius Josephus (*The Works of Flavius Josephus the Jewish Historian*, translated into English by William Whiston): *The Antiquities of the Jews*, Book XVIII 3.3, and Book XX 9.1, which mention Jesus in context as "Christ"; and XVIII 5.2, which mentions John the Baptist. All of these were written in the early 90s AD. Pliny the Younger, in *Epistulae* X.96, does not specifically mention Jesus, but the letter from Pliny, Governor of Bithynia et Pontus (now Turkey), to Roman Emperor Trajan written circa 112 A.D. seeks advice on how to deal with Christians being brought to him for trial because of their refusal to worship Roman gods. Cornelius Tacitus, in *Annals*, Book 15, Chapter 44, written circa 116 A.D., refers to Roman Emperor Nero's persecution of Christians following the great fire in Rome in 64 A.D., noting that Christians were followers of Christus, who had been executed in Judea during the reign of Emperor Tiberius.

outside the home of his childhood. Aramaic, a Semitic language closely related to Hebrew and which was common in the Middle East,[31] would have been the language used in his parents' home.[32]

Although the Greek-speaking (Hellenistic) Jews of Tarsus likely used the Greek translation of their Scriptures,[33] known as the Septuagint, in his youth Saul was sent to Jerusalem to experience a more orthodox religious education and spiritual formation, which would have been fulfilled in Aramaic.[34] Perhaps Saul's exposure to Greek culture as a boy was a contributing factor for his parents sending him to Jerusalem, the heart of Judaism. It would certainly be helpful to him later in life. In Jerusalem, Saul was privileged to be a student of Gamaliel, a chief leader of the Pharisees (Acts 5:34; 22:3).[35] A devoutly religious Jew, Saul *"was advancing in Judaism beyond many of [his] own age among [his] people, so extremely zealous was [he] for the traditions of [his] fathers"* (Galatians 1:14).

As an adult, Saul encountered and rejected the claim that Jesus was the Messiah.

But mere rejection was not enough for this fanatic of Judaism. Saul was determined to eradicate from the face of the earth those who believed and spread the false teaching (from his perspective) that Jesus of

---

31 Richard Gottheil and Wilhelm Bacher, "Aramaic Language Among the Jews," *Jewish Encyclopedia*. Date of access: November 8, 2018 (http://www.jewishencyclopedia.com/articles/1707–aramaic-language-among-the-jews).

32 C. Peter Wagner, *Acts of the Holy Spirit: A Modern Commentary on the Book of Acts* (Ventura, CA: Regal Books, A Division of Gospel Light, 2000), 181.

33 Christians call those Scriptures the Old Testament.

34 F.F. Bruce, *Paul: Apostle of the Heart Set Free* (Grand Rapids, MI: Chosen Books, 1991), 43.

35 *The ESV Study Bible* notes, "The Pharisees... were divided into at least three schools: the disciples of Shammai, Hillel, and Gamaliel... Gamaliel, the son (or grandson) of Hillel, was a renowned teacher of the law in Jerusalem." ("Jewish Groups at the Time of the New Testament," *The ESV Study Bible* [Wheaton, IL: Crossway, 2008], 1799–1800).

Nazareth was indeed the long-expected Anointed One of God, Saviour for the people of Israel.[36]

Stephen, a Hellenistic Jew who had become a Christ-follower, was arrested in Jerusalem for reason of his religious beliefs. At his trial before the Jewish community's ruling council, the Sanhedrin, Stephen shared a powerful testimony witnessing to his belief that Jesus was the Messiah (Acts 6:8–7:36). The crowd was enraged by Stephen's words! They carried Stephen outside the city walls and threw stones at him until he was dead (Acts 7:57–60). Supervising the crude execution was none other than Saul (Acts 7:58). More than just being present, *"Saul approved of his execution"* (Acts 8:1).

Saul began to destroy the church. Going from house to house, he dragged off both men and women and put them in prison (Acts 8:3).

As persecution increased in Jerusalem, Christians left the city and dispersed throughout the Roman Empire, carrying within them and sharing with others the message the Gospel of Jesus Christ (Acts 8:1, 4).

However, Saul continued to breathe murderous threats against the Lord's disciples. He went to the high priest and asked him for letters to the synagogues in Damascus, so that if he found any there who belonged to the Way (Christianity), whether men or women, he might take them as prisoners to Jerusalem (Acts 9:1–2).

Saul was the ideal candidate to seek and destroy followers of the Way. Able to speak and write in Aramaic and Greek, trained in the Scriptures, and zealous for the purity of Judaism, Saul was also a Roman citizen by birth (Acts 22:28–29), and he also likely incorporated some

---

[36] The name Jesus is the English version of the Greek transliteration *Iesous* (the word transliteration referring to the act of spelling a Greek word with English letters). There was no *J* in Greek, and the pronunciation was more of a *Y* sound, although we now use a hard *J* sound in English. The *Y* sound originates with the Hebrew/Aramaic name transliterated as *Yeshua*, which is the abbreviated version of *Yehoshua* (in English, this is usually rendered as Joshua and Jehoshua), which means "Yahweh [God] saves"; the abbreviated Yeshua/Joshua means "Saviour." See: James Strong, *Strong's Exhaustive Concordance: Greek Dictionary of the New Testament* (Grand Rapids, MI: Baker Book House, 1980), #2424, #3323, and #5547; James Strong, *Strong's Exhaustive Concordance: Hebrew and Chaldee Dictionary* (Grand Rapids, MI: Baker Book House, 1980), #3091 and #4899; and "Jesus Christ," *The Revell Bible Dictionary* (Grand Rapids, MI: Fleming H. Revell, 1990), 556.

Latin in his conversational skillset. His citizenship gave him rights others in Jerusalem might not have had, including freedom to travel throughout the Empire, freedom to hunt down and destroy the Way.

Saul was a model citizen of both a violent Empire and a virulent form of Judaism. There were leaders within both Empire and Judaism who felt somewhat threatened by the claims made by followers of the Way to having their own king (a rival to Caesar?) whom they also worshipped as the long-awaited Messiah, a rival to the religious and political power of the Jewish Sadducees and Pharisees.

Even today in the twenty-first century, we can find ourselves being like Saul—model citizens of our nation, devoted to a political cause. Christians might even aggressively oppose people and behaviours we are convinced the Bible says are wrong. Saul was an uncompromising constituent of the state and unflagging defender of his religion. He stood out among his peers. But beyond a few who joined him in crudely executing Stephen, how much influence did Saul have in first-century society?

Whether devoted to a political leader or a religious belief, one must wonder: is violence—even violent language, if not violent action—an effective means of enforcement to dissuade belief in Another? It didn't prove effective with the Way. Perhaps instead it bore out the truth in the words Gamaliel shared with the Sanhedrin at the trial of Peter and others of the Way who were arrested with him in Jerusalem's temple:

> *Men of Israel, take care what you are about to do with these men. For before these days Theudas rose up, claiming to be somebody, and a number of men, about four hundred, joined him. He was killed, and all who followed him were dispersed and came to nothing. After him Judas the Galilean rose up in the days of the census and drew away some of the people after him. He too perished, and all who followed him were scattered. So in the present case I tell you, keep away from these men and let them alone, for if this plan or this undertaking is of man, it will fail; but if it is of God, you will not be able to overthrow them. You might even be found opposing God!*
>
> —Acts 5:35–39

PART I: CHURCH

Accepting this sage advice, the Sanhedrin was merciful toward Jesus' followers. But what of Gamaliel's more volatile former student, Saul? Saul knew no such restraint. We will pick up his story in the next chapter.

Three Takeaways

- It pays to read the stuff before Chapter One, even the Acknowledgements.
- We are as capable of influencing our community of contact in the twenty-first century, for good or not-so-good, as Saul was in the first century.
- Saul of Tarsus was a model Roman citizen and enforcer of his religious beliefs.

CHAPTER TWO

PAUL OF TARSUS, CITIZEN MODEL

Now as he went on his way, he approached Damascus, and suddenly a light from heaven shone around him. And falling to the ground, he heard a voice saying to him, "Saul, Saul, why are you persecuting me?"

And he said, "Who are you, Lord?"

And he said, "I am Jesus, whom you are persecuting. But rise and enter the city, and you will be told what you are to do."

—Acts 9:3–6

My parents immigrated to Canada from Barbados in the 1950s. Although being Bajan meant they held citizenship of the United Kingdom and Colonies as well as that of Barbados, they prized Canadian citizenship and took the necessary steps to obtain it.

I, on the other hand, received my citizenship coincident with my birth at East York General Hospital in what is now part of Toronto. My elementary and secondary education in the Ontario public school system included Canadian history, basic rights of citizenship (civics), English (the language of my parents' home), and French (as a second language, English and French being Canada's official languages), among other subjects.

My encounter with Jesus was quiet, made within the safety of a nation that has a longstanding reputation for freedom of choice in religion. Relatively uncontroversial.

Saul the persecutor, on the other hand, had a spectacularly dramatic encounter with the resurrected Jesus—and he was living in a region and Empire that saw belief in the Messiah King as a threat, which Saul knew all too well. Controversy surrounded and influenced his life from the moment of his encounter onward. Here's that part of his story.

Armed with papers authorizing persecution of the Way, Saul headed out on the road from Jerusalem to Damascus, a journey of about 240 kilometres (150 miles), or two weeks on foot. Suddenly, Jesus, who had been crucified and whom Saul denied had risen from the dead, appeared before him and dropped Saul to his knees. The resurrected Jesus stood before Saul, challenged Saul's mission, and identified His followers as being His Body, a thought we'll return to in the next chapter. But first, more of Saul's experience (Acts 9:3–6; 1 Corinthians 15:8).

Saul was literally blinded by the light as Jesus, the Light of the World (John 8:12), stood before him to redirect the trajectory of Saul's life. Saul's travel companions had to take him by the hand in order to get him to Damascus. For three days, he neither ate nor drank anything.

In Damascus, Jesus had prepared another surprise. The Lord Jesus spoke to a Christ-follower there named Ananias, telling him to place his hands on Saul, restore his sight, and impart to Saul the Holy Spirit (Acts 9:7–19).

Jesus said to Ananias, *"Go! This man is my chosen instrument to proclaim my name to the Gentiles and their kings and to the people of Israel. I will show him how much he must suffer for my name"* (Acts 9:15–16, NIV). So Ananias went to where Saul was staying and prayed with him, as Jesus had said.

Saul, denier of Jesus and radical zealot for Judaism, set aside his plan in favour of God's plan. As a Christ-follower, he became known as Paul,[37] preeminent preacher of the Way and author or inspiration for more than half of the New Testament's books and letters.

That which had made *Saul* well-suited to be persecutor of the Way now positioned *Paul* as God's choice to proclaim the Gospel in word, both spoken and written, as well as deed, with his zeal tempered by compassion.

Raised and educated as a member of the Pharisee sect of Judaism, Paul received a thorough and scholarly education based in the Old Testament Scriptures. Part of the Pharisees' theology that enhanced Paul's ability to explain his encounter and relationship with Jesus was belief in

---

37   Paul was perhaps his Greek given name. In Latin, since he was a Roman citizen, it would have been Paulus.

the resurrection of the dead to an afterlife (Acts 23:6). Paul would also have been taught the Pharisees' belief in the combination of predestination (the belief that everything had been foreseen by God) and free will (the belief that all humans enjoy freedom of choice) that peppers his own writings,[38] a concept detectable in Gamaliel's comments to the Sanhedrin when Peter and others were on trial (Acts 5:34–39).

Perhaps most importantly, Paul would have known the certainty that God is One,[39] which was critical to his understanding and ability to explain the concept of God the Father, God the Son, and God the Holy Spirit as monotheistic, not polytheistic—One God, not three. Christianity, as it became known, was thus readily identified within its own body of believers as an authentic continuance of Judaism, adopting the Old Testament, which contained numerous prophecies of the Messiah as part of its own sacred writings. This gave Paul and other Christ-followers an historic and significant religious heritage.[40]

Another influential feature of Paul's theology for the early Church was the Pharisees' recognition of the value found in rabbinic expression and texts, including the spoken word tradition and writings of the great Jewish teachers. This motivated people's desire to keep a record of the words of Jesus as well as written instruction from Paul and others that would in time be agreed upon as the content of the New Testament.

Being a Roman citizen by birth meant that Paul's father had also been a Roman citizen. Whether inherited or secured at great cost, either

---

38 This is according to Flavius Josephus (*The Works of Flavius Josephus the Jewish Historian*, translated into English by William Whiston): *The Jewish War*, Book II 8.14; and *The Antiquities of the Jews*, Book XVIII 1.3 (http://penelope.uchicago.edu/josephus/index.html).

39 *"Hear, O Israel: The Lord our God, the Lord is one"* (Deuteronomy 6:4). This verse is referenced as the *Shema Yisrael*. See: James Strong, *Strong's Exhaustive Concordance, Hebrew and Chaldee Dictionary*, #8088 (*shema*, something heard); #8085 (*shama*, to hear intelligently, often with the implication of attention, obedience, etc.); and #8086 (*sh'ma*, to hear, obey). See also: Larry W. Hurtado, *Destroyer of the gods: Early Christian Distinctiveness in the Roman World* (Waco, TX: Baylor University Press, 2016), 71–72.

40 Christianity was originally perceived to be a sect of Judaism. This contributed to the objection of Jewish leaders to the claim that Jesus was the long-awaited Messiah. It is also why the admission of Gentile God-fearers into the ranks of the Way, without requiring adherence to Jewish traditions, was controversial in the early days of the Church (Acts 10, 15:1–29). See also: Hurtado, *Destroyer of the gods*, 109–111.

in battle or by substantial financial payment, Roman citizenship was a status valued above all else in the Empire. In addition to Aramaic and Greek, Paul likely had at least a working knowledge and capacity in Latin, the language of Rome.[41] As a citizen, he would likely have been educated in Roman history and law, Greek history and philosophy, and the Jewish history, religious law, and sacred text that were integral to his family heritage.

Combined with his dramatic conversion experience, Paul's education, citizenship, and language skills made him an ideal candidate to be selected by the Holy Spirit (Acts 13:1–3) to travel throughout the Roman Empire to preach the Gospel, encourage Christians dispersed by the persecution taking place in Jerusalem, and establish new congregations of Christ-followers.

Over the course of three expeditions, Paul travelled by land and sea through much of modern Syria, Turkey, Greece, Cyprus, and Lebanon. In the course of those travels, Paul planted or watered (1 Corinthians 3:6) dozens of churches before heading to a meeting in Jerusalem.

While in Jerusalem, he was arrested in the temple for being a follower of the Way (Acts 21:33). As the frenzied crowd sought to kill Paul, he was whisked into custody. Before Paul could be flogged for the disturbance his presence had generated, he revealed himself to the Roman commander to be a Roman citizen (Acts 22:25–28), not someone who could encounter the force of the *flagrum*[42] without a trial, unless the commander himself wanted to face the penalty of law.

In prison awaiting trial, Paul heard of about forty men conspiring to kill him before he could get to the Roman court. Paul revealed the plot to his jailers and the commander ordered a massive bodyguard for Paul's journey to court: two hundred soldiers, two hundred spearmen, seventy horsemen, and mounts for both Paul and the commander, who accompanied him personally to the governor (Acts 22:12–24). American pastor, educator, and author Chuck Swindoll wrote,

---

41 John Pollock, *The Apostle: A Life of Paul* (Colorado Springs, CO: David C. Cook, 2011), 16.

42 A *flagrum* was a multi-strap whip with objects tied to its belts to enhance the damage inflicted.

Uniformed, armed, and trained soldiers. Four-hundred seventy-two to forty rag-tag conspirators. Nice odds. *Talk about overkill.* The guy would not be outdone. He made sure no one could get to Paul.[43]

Citizenship has its rights! Paul knew it. So did the Roman commander, and he wasn't about to let a Roman citizen under his care be assassinated by twoscore of hostile zealots from a virulent sect of Judaism.

If Paul hadn't known the rights of his citizenship, and exercised them, we could easily be missing half of the books in the New Testament, books either written or influenced because of Paul's survival, imprisonment, and then journey to Rome based on his right, as a Roman citizen, to be tried before Caesar.

There is speculation that Paul spent time in prison while in Ephesus on his third missionary journey, prior to his arrest in Jerusalem. From prison in Ephesus, he may have written two letters, Philemon and Philippians.[44] Often, however, those two letters are included in the following list of texts which were probably written after the Jerusalem conspiracy: 2 Corinthians, Ephesians, Philippians, Colossians, Philemon, 1 Timothy, 2 Timothy, Titus, and Hebrews.[45] The Gospel of Luke and Book of Acts,

---

[43] Charles R. Swindoll, *Paul: A Man of Grace and Grit: Profiles in Character* (Nashville, TN: Thomas Nelson, 2002), 255.

[44] Paul states that these letters were written from prison in Philemon 10 and Philippians 1:12–14. The timing may have been during the three years Paul spent in Ephesus (Acts 20:31), part of which time he may have been in prison. Paul notes multiple imprisonments in 2 Corinthians 11:23 but does not specify where they were. See: Benjamin W. Robinson, "An Ephesian Imprisonment of Paul," *Journal of Biblical Literature*, Volume 29, Number 2 (1910): 181–89 (http://www.jstor.org/stable/4617113); and Marcus J. Borg, *Evolution of the Word: The New Testament in the Order the Books Were Written* (New York, NY: HarperCollins Publishers, 2012), 85, 91.

[45] Although there is some question about the authorship of Hebrews, which may have merely been written in the Pauline style.

both letters to Luke's friend or patron Theophilus,[46] were also likely dependent on Paul's input and written after his imprisonment.[47] [48]

Years later, Peter, who had the benefit of reading at least some of Paul's letters and considered them to be authoritative, made this statement:

> *Therefore, beloved, since you are waiting for these, be diligent to be found by him without spot or blemish, and at peace. And count the patience of our Lord as salvation, just as our beloved brother Paul also wrote to you according to the wisdom given him, as he does in all his letters when he speaks in them of these matters. There are some things in them that are hard to understand, which the ignorant and unstable twist to their own destruction, as they do the other Scriptures.*
> —2 Peter 3:14–16 (see also Ephesians 5:27)[49]

Paul knew that the rights of his Roman citizenship applied equally to him, even as a Christian, as much as for any other citizen of the Empire. After his Damascus road encounter with Jesus, Paul didn't use those rights for his own benefit, but for the sake of the Gospel.

Saul may have been the model citizen of the violent Roman Empire and a virulent strain of Judaism. Paul, however, was a citizen model for Christians of the first and twenty-first centuries alike, utilizing the advantages of his citizenship for diplomatic Gospel witness to constituents and leaders of the first-century Roman world. And surprisingly, as

---

46   Theophilus is the English transliteration of a Greek word or name that means "friend of God."
47   Kat Cendana, "The Letters of Paul," *Amazing Bible Timeline with World History*. November 18, 2016 (https://amazingbibletimeline.com/blog/paul-the-letters-of); and "Chronology of Acts and the Epistles," *Blue Letter Bible*. Date of access: November 17, 2018 (https://www.blueletterbible.org/study/pnt/pnt02.cfm).
48   In *Evolution of the Word*, Borg sets out a potential chronological order of the Pauline and Pauline-influenced books of the New Testament: 1 Thessalonians, Galatians, 1 Corinthians, Philemon, Philippians, 2 Corinthians, Romans, Colossians, Hebrews, Ephesians, Luke, Acts, 2 Thessalonians, 1 Timothy, 2 Timothy, and Titus. Borg notes differing opinions on dating each book/letter and the reasons he settled on this order.
49   Hurtado notes that Peter refers to a "collection of Pauline epistles" and that "this may have been the earliest step toward the larger collection that we know as the New Testament" (Hurtado, *Destroyer of the gods*, 114).

a leader in an outcast religion, Paul had far more influence on his culture and society than Saul ever had.

That which prepared Paul for his life before his encounter with Jesus was part of his preparation to live his life *for* Jesus. In that way, Paul's not so different from you or me. All of our life experiences prepare us for life as Christ-followers, including the state-defined characteristics of our earthly citizenship, whether that citizenship was earned by testing or granted by birth, and the commission of our heavenly citizenship in Jesus.

Three Takeaways

- Everyone has a past. It got us to where Jesus loves us, and to where He can work with and through us today.
- The Pharisees were not as bad as we sometimes say they were. In fact, their theology proved essential to each Christian's understanding of what it means to follow Jesus.
- Knowing your rights of citizenship equips you to better share the Gospel.

CHAPTER THREE

THE CHURCH, PEOPLE OF THE WORD

> *All Scripture is breathed out by God and profitable for teaching, for reproof, for correction, and for training in righteousness, that the man [or woman, i.e. messenger] of God may be complete, equipped for every good work.*
>
> —2 Timothy 3:16–17

I remember getting a Gideon's New Testament in public school in Grade Five, and signing the decision page at the back, much like everyone else in the class, at least to my knowledge. Some days I wonder how reading and signing that page influenced my life. But I didn't start reading the Bible in any meaningful way until my second year of university when the group I was in studied the Gospel of Mark. That was the year I received the awesome Bible that my aunt and uncle gave me for Christmas in 1979.

In time, I read that Bible from cover to cover, with seemingly no effect. But

> *the word of God is living and active, sharper than any two-edged sword, piercing to the division of soul and of spirit, of joints and of marrow, and discerning the thoughts and intentions of the heart. And no creature is hidden from his sight, but all are naked and exposed to the eyes of him to whom we must give account.*
>
> —Hebrews 4:12–13

It was in November 1981, a few months after I started attending a church, that I began to seriously contemplate whether I was a Christian. The content of that Christmas Bible was a gamechanger after I became a Christian on December 5, 1981, and its reading over the two years prior was instrumental in my commitment to Jesus.

When Paul wrote to Timothy about the profitability of Scripture, he was writing about what Christians today call the Old Testament. The story of God, creation, humanity, and redemption through a promised and prophesied Saviour—the Messiah, the Christ—was all readily found in the Old Testament. I don't think Paul suspected that one day his letter to a protégé would be included in Scripture. But as we saw in the previous chapter, Peter recognized the importance of Paul's letters to the young Church.

Some suggest that the 323 A.D. Council of Nicea determined the contents of the Old and New Testaments. However, it is generally accepted that what the council did was affirm the texts that were already broadly accepted within the Church. The primary discussion at the council was not to assess Scripture but to address a difference in teaching that had arisen about Jesus. The council affirmed Jesus as both Son of God *and* Son of Man.

Scottish biblical historian F.F. Bruce tells us more about the text we today accept as the Old and New Testaments:

> The first ecclesiastical councils to classify the canonical books were both held in North Africa—at Hippo Regius in 393 and at Carthage in 397—but what these councils did was not to impose something new upon the Christian communities but to codify what was already the general practice of these communities.[50]

There are lists of authoritative writings that were assembled by individuals at earlier dates,[51] but these councils are considered definitive as

---

50 F.F. Bruce, *The New Testament Documents: Are They Reliable?* (Grand Rapids, MI: Eerdmans, 1960), 27.
51 Hurtado, *Destroyer of the gods*, 111–118.

they brought together an assembly of the recognized senior Christian leaders of the era who acknowledged content that was and continues to be accepted.

When I visited Nigeria in 2011, we distributed about four hundred Bibles to people who had lost theirs in the anti-Christian violence following the presidential election. When I say lost, some were left behind, but many were deliberately destroyed by the attackers. One woman knelt before me in tears as I handed her a replacement for her lost treasure. I dropped to my knees in front of her before placing it in her hands. Then, taking her free hand, we stood up together, equal, brother and sister in Christ. She shared with me the immeasurable value it was for her to again have a Bible she could read on a daily basis.

Here's an inspiring true story about Bibles in China:

> In November 2015, I was privileged to travel to China to visit the world's largest Bible printing facility and to have conversations with leaders of the state-registered Protestant and Catholic churches. In 2006 and 2008, I had met in Canada and the U.S. respectively with leaders from China's unregistered church movement. Both sides of the Chinese Church, registered and unregistered, shared something: a key catalyst to their growth has been obtaining, reading, studying, and discussing the printed Word of God in their own language. One result of this growth and study has been that every province of China now has Christian social services serving the neediest of the nation. On a beautiful evening in Nanjing, we enjoyed cake prepared in a Christian bakery staffed by the developmentally disabled.[52]

---

52   Hutchinson, *Under Siege*, 221.

Established in 1985 and printing Bibles since 1987, the Amity Printing Company is a joint project between The Amity Foundation,[53] which is China's first faith-based and now largest charity, and the United Bible Societies. Amity Printing has printed more than one hundred million Bibles—not including paperback New Testaments and other Bible portions—for global distribution and another eighty million in Chinese.[54]

During my 2015 visit, representing the Canadian Bible Society as part of a delegation from the United Bible Societies, Lane Dennis from Crossway Books was present to sign the agreement that resulted in publication of a Chinese Study Bible based on the *ESV Study Bible*.[55] We were privileged to be gifted copies of the New Testament Study Bible fresh off the press. The complete Chinese Study Bible with Old Testament and New Testament was released in December 2017.[56] Look through an *ESV Study Bible* and imagine the significance of this resource to Chinese Christians and their leaders.

The Scriptures are still powerful, profitable for Christian discipleship, and preparatory for Christian service.

> The gospel message requires us as Christ-followers to identify more than one or two Bible verses that we have interpreted to support our thoughts. We are called to acquire an understanding of the overarching theme of the Bible, and then engage in what the apostle Paul calls *"the ministry of reconciliation"* (2 Corinthians 5:18). Not one dot on an "i" or horizontal line on

---

53 The Amity Foundation was established by Bishop K.H. Ting in 1985. Amity provides a variety of social service ministries, including medical clinics, disaster relief, financial support for orphans and education for those living in poverty, a blindness prevention program, community-based elder care, ministries to people with disabilities (including the Amity Children's Centre), support to start-up NGOs and capacity building, and international Christian service volunteer opportunities. See: *The Amity Foundation: 30th Anniversary, Footprints of Love* (Nanjing, JS: The Amity Foundation, 2015).

54 "Scripture Impact Since 1985," *United Bible Societies China Partnership*. Date of access: January 2, 2018 (https://www.ubscp.org/scripture-impact).

55 Lane T. Dennis and Wayne Grudem, eds., *The ESV Study Bible* (Wheaton, IL: Crossway, 2008).

56 "Launch of the Chinese Study Bible," *United Bible Societies China Partnership*. January 17, 2018 (https://www.ubscp.org/launch-chinese-studybible).

a "t" will disappear from the Old Testament. But for our righteousness to be greater than that of ancient religious leaders who insisted on adherence to all the Old Testament laws, and the laws they built upon those laws, we need to embrace the whole gospel, the full story that includes creation, the fall of humanity, wandering, redemption, and restoration in Christ. Into that story fits our pursuit of justice.

To learn and live a whole gospel life requires effort on our part...

I encourage you to begin by investing in your understanding of the gospel, set in the whole context of Scripture. Like any other interest you might pursue in life, it's worth making a small expenditure to really get into it. And this investment isn't just about a hobby; it's your life.[57]

First, get your hands on a Bible you will read.

Over the decades, I have used several Bibles and continue to benefit from them. That first Bible from Texas, *The Open Bible*, was the New American Standard Bible translation and it was also a study Bible.[58] Beyond the text, the notes helped me to better understand some of the things the Bible had to say. My next Bible was the New International Version translation, and also a study Bible, called the *Thompson Chain-Reference Bible*.[59] The linking of verses in the Thompson Chain shows how the Bible supports itself. This fuelled my interest in Bible reading and study even more.

One thing has remained consistent in my selection of Bibles over the years: my daily go-to Bible has to feel right in my hands and to my eyes. I like to touch and feel a Bible before I buy it, to get a sense that I'm going to enjoy picking it up, opening it, and delving into its contents daily. I like my study Bibles to open flat on a desk or table.

---

57 Hutchinson, *Under Siege*, 132–133.
58 *New American Standard Bible: The Open Bible Edition* (Nashville, TN: Thomas Nelson, Publishers, 1979).
59 Frank Charles Thompson, ed., *The Thompson Chain Reference Bible: New International Version* (Indianapolis, IN: B.B. Kirkbride Bible Co., Inc., 1983).

PART I: CHURCH

The congregation we're part of uses the English Standard Version for readings and for our Bible School, so I purchased a go-to ESV Bible. For eight dollars, I purchased an ESV Deluxe Compact Bible with a minor defect in how some of the pages were cut. I like it because it has clear print and it's pocket-size. I read from it daily. You don't have to spend a lot of money to get the right Bible for you.

What's the best Bible? Which translation is best? The one you will read. I have read several translations and paraphrases, along with complaints theologians have about every single one of them![60]

The chart below was printed in *Under Siege* to assist those assessing different translations. The Bible for you may be what your congregation is using, one that just feels right to you, or the only Bible available where you are. They're all good!

Types of Bible Translations

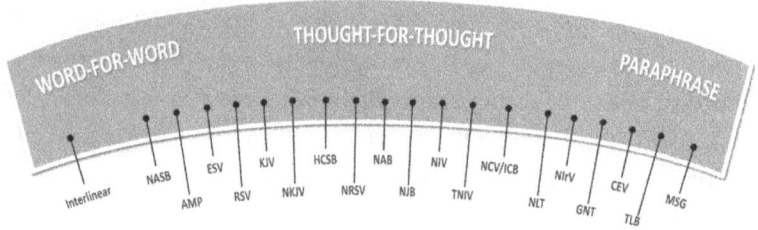

NASB: New American Standard Bible
AMP: Amplified Bible
ESV: English Standard Version
RSV: Revised Standard Version
KJV: King James Version
NKJV: New King James Version

HCSB: Holman Christian Standard Bible
NRSV: New Revised Standard Version
NAB: New American Bible
NJB: New Jerusalem Bible
NIV: New International Version
NCV/ICB: New Century Version / International Children's Bible
NLT: New Living Translation
TNIV: Today's New International Version

NIrV: New International Reader's Version
GNT: Good News Translation (also Good News Bible)
CEV: Contemporary English Version
TLB: The Living Bible
MSG: The Message

After you have a Bible that suits you, invest in some resources to help you study it for yourself.

---

60   Hutchinson, *Under Siege*, 133.

Equip yourself to examine the Scriptures, to test what others tell you and follow the truth. You don't need a large library, just a few good books.

You may want a Bible with study notes, like *The Open Bible* or *Thompson Chain-Reference Bible*. Another popular Bible in the Pentecostal movement[61] is the *Fire Bible*.[62] There are lots of Bibles with good study notes.

If, like me, you are using a Bible that is text-only, you might want to pick up a study Bible. Study Bibles include the biblical text and often have more notes and commentary than Bibles with complementary study notes, such as those mentioned in the paragraph above. As mentioned, our congregation uses the ESV as our teaching Bible, and the ESV Study Bible as a reference resource in our Bible school.

Some good books that will be of benefit to you in understanding your faith and your Bible are *Knowing God* by J.I. Packer[63] and *What the Bible Is All About* by Henrietta Mears.[64] Both have been popular for decades, are available in inexpensive paperback versions, and are readily found in stores that carry Christian books.

Knowing God is a good book to learn key principles for the Christian life. It's divided topically and includes Bible references in the text. Packer, an English-born Canadian, has long been regarded as one of the world's preeminent evangelical theologians.

What the Bible Is All About is a book-by-book overview of the Bible for adults, written by an American Sunday school teacher who taught the material first. Billy Graham used to give this book to new Christians at his crusades.

To encourage you in the development of a daily Bible-reading habit, I also recommend acquiring a daily devotional. Devotionals present a

---

61 There are now more than four hundred fifty million Pentecostals alive today, of the nearly two and a half billion Christians. See: "Status of Global Christianity, 2019, in the Context of 1900–2050," *Gordon Conwell Theological Seminary*. Date of access: September 19, 2019 (https://gordonconwell.edu/wp-content/uploads/sites/13/2019/04/StatusofGlobalChristianity20191.pdf).

62 Donald C. Stamps, ed., *Fire Bible: English Standard Version* (Peabody, MA: Hendrickson Publishers Marketing LLC, 2014).

63 J.I. Packer, *Knowing God* (Downers Grove, IL: Intervarsity Press, 1973).

64 Henrietta Mears, *What the Bible Is All About* (Ventura, CA: Regal Books, 1985). First edition 1953.

daily Bible verse or passage to reflect on and a brief thought or commentary on the passage to help focus your thoughts. My first daily devotional was a first-Christmas-together gift from my wife Gloria in 1982. *My Utmost for His Highest* by Oswald Chambers[65] is a devotional classic, first published in 1924, that I used for several years and still revisit every three to five years.

You can also find interesting daily devotionals, study notes, and Bibles in electronic formats, such as the *YouVersion*[66] Bible app.

Check with your pastor or spiritual mentor to find out if he or she would suggest other helpful resources.

Chuck Swindoll recommends getting an exhaustive Bible concordance and a Bible dictionary when you're ready for serious Bible study.[67] Swindoll also recommends a Bible atlas and Bible commentary, but a good study Bible will include commentary and maps.

> You don't need bookcases full of Christian books. If you can swing it, you'll benefit from a half-shelf of books you'll read and use as a continuing resource for understanding the narrative of the whole context of the Bible, and the issues of life.[68]

For the Christian, there is no substitute for reading and studying the Bible as the foundation for exploring, understanding, and expressing Christianity as a life orientation, both in terms of belief and behaviour. Scottish New Testament scholar and early Christianity historian Larry Hurtado notes that "reading and discussing scripture texts" was "a regular part of early Christian corporate worship."[69] In Acts, Luke states, as Paul did to Timothy in 2 Timothy 3:16–17, the value to be found in knowing and studying the Scriptures.

---

65 Oswald Chambers, *My Utmost for His Highest: Selections for the Year* (New York, NY: Dodd, Mead & Company, 1935).
66 The YouVersion Bible app can he found here: https://www.youversion.com.
67 Charles R. Swindoll, "Tools," *Insight for Living Ministries*. April 26, 2015 (https://www.insight.org/resources/daily-devotional/individual/tools).
68 Hutchinson, *Under Siege*, 135.
69 Hurtado, *Destroyer of the gods*, 109.

> *The brothers [and sisters] immediately sent Paul and Silas away by night to Berea, and when they arrived they went into the Jewish synagogue. Now these Jews were more noble than those in Thessalonica; they received the word with all eagerness, examining the Scriptures daily to see if these things were so. Many of them therefore believed, with not a few Greek women of high standing as well as men.*
>
> —Acts 17:10–12

Receive the Word with all eagerness. Examine the Scriptures daily. Study to know whether what someone claims to be true is, in fact, true.

Do these things and you will be equipped to live a noble Christian life, regardless of your circumstance. An intimate relationship with God and with Scripture is vital to living a life of Christian influence and Christian citizenship.

Three Takeaways

- To live a life of Christian citizenship, we need to understand what it is to be a Christian.
- The Bible tells God's story, and ours. It inspires, without manipulating, and is the guide for our lives with Jesus and with others.
- It is helpful to have a Bible you feel good about reading, and to read from it regularly (perhaps with a few inexpensive but helpful resources to help your understanding) in order to grasp the big picture painted by its words.

CHAPTER FOUR

THE CHURCH, MANY PARTS, ONE BODY

I do not ask for these only, but also for those who will believe in me through their word, that they may all be one, just as you, Father, are in me, and I in you, that they also may be in us, so that the world may believe that you have sent me.

—John 17:20–21

For as in one body we have many members, and the members do not all have the same function, so we, though many, are one body in Christ, and individually members one of another.

—Romans 12:4–5

But God has so composed the body, giving greater honor to the part that lacked it, that there may be no division in the body, but that the members may have the same care for one another. If one member suffers, all suffer together; if one member is honored, all rejoice together.
Now you are the body of Christ and individually members of it.

—1 Corinthians 12:24–27

IN JANUARY 2014, I MADE MY FIRST TRIP TO ISRAEL AS PART OF A DELEGATION travelling with Canada's Prime Minister, Stephen Harper. The official part of the visit was sandwiched between captivating meetings I had with representatives from different parts of the Body of Christ in the Holy Land. These meetings were an example for me of the biblical concept of *many parts, one Body.*

On the evening of the day I arrived, I had the pleasure of meeting in Jerusalem with leaders from the evangelical Christian community.

The next day, I journeyed with Andrew Bennett, Canada's Ambassador for Religious Freedom and a member of the Ukrainian Greek-Catholic Church, on the Via Dolorosa. As part of our time, we reflected on meetings with leaders from various Christian denominations who live in Jerusalem. We shared meditations prepared by Pope John Paul II at the Stations of the Cross, and the walk concluded at the Church of the Holy Sepulchre, which is jointly maintained by the Greek Orthodox, Armenian Apostolic, and Roman Catholic denominations, with lesser participation by the Coptic Orthodox, Syriac Orthodox, and Ethiopian Orthodox expressions of Christianity. Protestant denominations have no official role in the care of that particular church building, but not far away is the Anglican Christ Church Jerusalem, with a guest house, also within the walls of the Old City.

That evening, I enjoyed worship with a Pentecostal congregation, in Hebrew and English, in their building near the Yehuda Market.

The day following the official part of the trip, I met with several Arab Christian leaders in Bethlehem, in what is most often referred to as the West Bank, on the other side of the security fence/wall.

Returning to Jerusalem, I attended a service that evening with one of the Arab Christian leaders and his family at an evangelical church that worships in Arabic, with the English translation whispered in my ear to make sure I felt welcome. We were meeting in the oldest evangelical congregation in Jerusalem, literally in the upper room of a building reached by walking along a back alley in a residential neighbourhood inside the city wall.

One Body. Many parts.

While our imaginations are within the walls of the Old City of Jerusalem, let's wander down an alley where today's walls and narrow roads are made of centuries-old limestone, put in place long before the birth of Jesus, then into a first-century upper room. Let me share some relevant words from *Under Siege*:

On the night He was betrayed, Jesus washed His disciples' feet. For them it was a disquieting experience of loving service. The disciples understood the role of a house servant to wash the dusty feet of guests, but the paradigm shift of having their feet washed by their Master Rabbi, the Son of God, left some speechless.

One refused the service, until he understood its purpose. Afterward Jesus challenged them, and us, with a new commandment:

A new commandment I give to you, that you love one another: just as I have loved you, you also are to love one another. By this all people will know that you are my disciples, if you have love for one another.
—John 13:34–35

This was a clear message about Christ-follower loving Christ-follower as a witness to those outside the Church.

Later in the evening, Jesus prayed for our unity, that we *"may all be one, just as you, Father, are in me, and I in you, that they also may be in us, so that the world may believe that you have sent me"* (John 17:21).

Jesus knew our diversity would be just as great as, and greater than, that of the twelve in the upper room with Him. It's not about sameness. Unity is our diversity collected in common purpose. That may involve divergent expressions and pursuits, but with the common purpose of bringing glory to God. May our pursuits be based not purely in personal preference, or theological sameness, but in kingdom purpose. His purpose.

A well-known Latin phrase reads, *In necessariis unitas, in non necessariis libertas, in utrusque caritas* ("In essentials, there should be unity; in non-essentials, liberty; in both cases, charity [love]"). The origins of this phrase have been attributed variously to Augustine, Bishop of Hippo Regius in North Africa, who is recognized as a saint by both Roman Catholics and

Anglicans; Rupertus Meldenius, a Lutheran theologian who taught in the German university city of Augsburg; and others. No attribution is required to recognize that this simple statement defines the starting point of effective engagement for Christians with each other. First, let us discontinue the quarrelling about who belongs in the Body of Christ because we may disagree on non-essentials. Beyond the essentials, there needs to be a demonstration of grace. We can, do, and will have conversations about our differences, but let them be civil conversations, grounded in love. Some will judge this a most liberal understanding of theological divisions. Others will deem it a starkly conservative interpretation of the red letters found in some Bibles, the words of Jesus.

The price of admission to the Church was paid on a cross on Mount Calvary. It makes no difference whether one belongs to a church that focuses on being able to state the date and time of one's decision to follow Christ or a church in which members cannot remember a moment in life when they didn't aspire to do so. What matters is that we do desire to follow Him.[70]

Our personal relationship and/or experience with Jesus may convince us that our congregation or denomination has got it right. Our theological differences and variances in worship style or expression may cause us to think other Christians have got it wrong. They may feel similarly about us, that they're right and we're wrong.

Jesus and Paul remind us that *they* are *us* and *we* are *them*. Distinct parts. Same Body.

The shared life of the Body of Christ was a cornerstone of Paul's ministry. Remember, when he met Jesus on the road to Damascus, Jesus' question to Saul/Paul was, *"Saul, Saul, why are you persecuting me?"* Saul asked, *"Who are you, Lord?"* Jesus answered, *"I am Jesus, whom you are persecuting"* (Acts 9:4–5). The face-to-face experience with Jesus that resulted in Paul becoming a Christ-follower imprinted on Paul the one Body

---

70   Hutchinson, *Under Siege*, 224–225.

concept. Saul thought he was pursuing Christians, but instead he was dramatically confronted with the truth that he was persecuting Christ.

Different gifts. One Body. A diversity of leadership. The building of one Body (Romans 12:3–5; 1 Corinthians 12; Ephesians 4:1–16).

I wonder if Paul reflected on the death of Stephen, and how often? Perhaps Jesus' words on the Damascus road gave Paul a revised perspective on the significance of Stephen, the table server (Acts 6:1–5) to widows and orphans (James 1:27), whose death he had supervised (Act 7:57–60), maybe even instigated.

It was because of his identification with the one Body of Christ, including a newfound appreciation for the needs Stephen had been serving, that Paul was several years later in Jerusalem when he was arrested.

At present, however, I am going to Jerusalem bringing aid to the saints. For Macedonia and Achaia have been pleased to make some contribution for the poor among the saints at Jerusalem.

—Romans 15:25–26

Paul understood that the one Body concept was about more than spiritual gifts and numeric growth—growth that continues to this day, with nearly half of Canada's twenty-two million self-declared Christians[71] meeting in congregations with an attendance of seventy-five people or less,[72] just one portion of the nearly two and a half billion Christians around the world, which had a population of 7.3 billion people in 2015.[73] One Body awareness is indispensably linked to meeting needs within the Church as a practical demonstration of love for one another.

---

71   "Two-Thirds of Population Declare Christian as Their Religion," *Statistics Canada*. February 19, 2016 (https://www150.statcan.gc.ca/n1/pub/91-003-x/2014001/section03/33-eng.htm).

72   "Church Attendance," *Outreach Canada*, June 27, 2016 (https://www.outreach.ca/resources/research/ArticleId/613/Church-Attendance).

73   "The Changing Global Religious Landscape," *Pew Research Centre*. April 5, 2017 (http://www.pewforum.org/2017/04/05/the-changing-global-religious-landscape). See also: "Status of Global Christianity, 2019, in the Context of 1900–2050," *Gordon Conwell Theological Seminary*. Date of access: September 20, 2019 (https://gordonconwell.edu/wp-content/uploads/sites/13/2019/04/StatusofGlobalChristianity20191.pdf).

In his book *Heirloom Love*, Dominic Sputo, an American advocate for the poor and persecuted, sets this scene from Paul's time:

> According to Acts, there were apparently more than ten thousand believers in Jesus by the time of Stephen's martyrdom [endnoted in *Heirloom Love* are Acts 2:41, 47; 4:4; 5:14; 6:1, 7]. Imagine the multiple hardships implied when we read that "they were all scattered" throughout the surrounding regions. Fleeing for their lives, thousands of families left behind their homes, their livelihoods, their extended families and support networks. Today in the West, we can fall back on temporary housing and on help to find new employment. But these people literally faced a life-and-death quandary as they attempted to resettle in strange lands. Who would come to their aid? The uncaring Roman government? No. The majority of fellow Jews, who disbelieved the claims of Jesus? No. They were dependent solely on the mercy of other Jesus followers to provide them with food and shelter.[74]

Paul wrote that in the Body of Christ there *"is neither Jew nor Greek, there is neither slave nor free, there is no male and female, for you are all one in Christ Jesus"* (Galatians 3:28). American New Testament scholar and author Jeremiah Johnston tells us,

> From Roman and Jewish perspectives, every part of this astonishing declaration is problematic.
> In Paul's time, people were divided by race, by free or slave status, and by gender. What Paul says in his letter that circulated among the churches he founded in the region of Galatia in Asia Minor (today's Turkey) would have been flatly rejected by the vast majority of the inhabitants of the Roman Empire,

---

[74] Dominic Sputo, with Brian Smith, *Heirloom Love: Authentic Christianity for This Age of Persecution* (Canada: Dominic Sputo, 2016), 28–29.

including the Jewish people. Many would have thought Paul's ideas laughable.[75]

Paul called on those who grasped the one Body message to pray for and contribute financially to the aid of their brothers and sisters, their family in Christ, regardless of social status or who was in need. He also made sure those who received this charitable assistance knew that it was being provided from equal to equal within the Body, not greater to lesser. A significant component in Paul's travels was the collection of financial support for the suffering Christians in Jerusalem and area. He encouraged generous, cheerful giving for this cause (Romans 15:25–27; 1 Corinthians 16:1–4; 2 Corinthians 8–9).

It was in Jerusalem, after delivering a collection for the saints in need, that Paul was arrested (Acts 21; 24:17), beginning the in-custody journey that would lead him to Rome.

Jesus, too, had been arrested in Jerusalem. We know well the story of His arrest, crucifixion, and resurrection. But how well do we understand the message He shared about loving one another, within the Church?

As we turn our thoughts to some familiar words from Jesus, let's adopt the one Body mindset of Paul, whose perspective was forever changed the moment he grasped that he was hunting Jesus when he hounded Christians.

> *While he was still speaking to the people, behold, his mother and his brothers stood outside, asking to speak to him. But he replied to the man who told him, "Who is my mother, and who are my brothers?"* ***And stretching out his hand toward his disciples, he said, "Here are my mother and my brothers! For whoever does the will of my Father in heaven is my brother and sister and mother."***
>
> —Matthew 12:46–50 (emphasis added)

> *Then the King will say to those on his right, "Come, you who are blessed by my Father, inherit the kingdom prepared for you from the*

---

[75] Jeremiah J. Johnston, *Unimaginable: What Our World Would Be Like Without Christianity* (Minneapolis, MN: Bethany House Publishers, 2017), 52.

> *foundation of the world. For I was hungry and you gave me food, I was thirsty and you gave me drink, I was a stranger and you welcomed me, I was naked and you clothed me, I was sick and you visited me, I was in prison and you came to me."*
>
> *Then the righteous will answer him, saying, "Lord, when did we see you hungry and feed you, or thirsty and give you drink? And when did we see you a stranger and welcome you, or naked and clothe you? And when did we see you sick or in prison and visit you?"*
>
> *And the King will answer them, "Truly, I say to you,* **as you did it to one of the least of these my brothers [and sisters], you did it to me."**
>
> —Matthew 25:34–40 (emphasis added)

We are irrefutably called to minister to the one Body, our brothers and sisters in Christ. John, the beloved disciple, put it this way:

> *We know that we have passed out of death into life, because we love the brothers… By this we know love, that he laid down his life for us, and we ought to lay down our lives for the brothers. But if anyone has the world's goods and sees his brother in need, yet closes his heart against him, how does God's love abide in him? Little children, let us not love in word or talk but in deed and in truth.*
>
> —1 John 3:14, 16–18

This is what love looks like in the one Church of many congregations in many cities from many nationalities. Those who *have* give from what they have, spiritual and material, to help those who *have not*, even those they have never met.

Peter, who had vouched for the authority of Paul's words, was present in the upper room when Jesus gave His disciples the new commandment, stating it five times that evening (John 13:34–35; 15:12, 17).

Peter also embraced this perspective as a cornerstone of his ministry. In 1 Peter 4:8, he writes, *"Above all, keep loving[76] one another earnestly…"*
Above all! Keep loving one another! Earnestly!
Sputo writes,

> Love for fellow believers is an ongoing theme throughout Peter's letter; just as he mentioned his readers' suffering in every chapter, so also in every chapter he exhorted them to love each other (1:22; 2:17; 3:8; 4:8; 5:14). Peter would never deny the importance of loving unbelievers; after all, he walked beside the Master Himself and watched Jesus loving every type of person He encountered. But again we see a priority on showing love toward each other within the worldwide body of Christ.[77]

We are called to minister as the Body of Christ *to* the Body of Christ, to love one another. It was a vital component of Jesus' last words for His disciples on the evening of His betrayal, and a theme repeated by several authors in the epistles of the New Testament.

We are also called to minister *as* the Body of Christ to those *outside* the Body of Christ—to love one another and to love our neighbours. It's a both/and reality, not an either/or one.

---

76 The word Peter uses here for "loving" is the same word for "love" attributed to Jesus in John 13:34–35, quoted above, and that John used in the quote above from 1 John 3—*agape*. See: James Strong, *Strong's Exhaustive Concordance, Greek Dictionary of the New Testament,* #25 (*agapao*), #26 (*agape*), meaning much affection or benevolence in a social or moral sense. In his book *The Four Loves* (Glasgow, UK: William Collins and Co Ltd, 1979), C.S. Lewis refers to *agape* as "divine Gift-love": "He communicates to men a share of His own Gift-love. This is different from the Gift-loves He has built into their own nature… Divine Gift-love—Love Himself working in man—is wholly disinterested and desires what is simply best for the beloved. Again, natural Gift-love is always directed to objects which the lover finds in some way intrinsically lovable… But Divine Gift-love in man enables him to love what is not naturally lovable; lepers, criminals, enemies, morons, the sulky, the superior and the sneering…" (117). Some, particularly earlier, translations into English use the word *charity* for *agape* love.

77 Sputo, *Heirloom Love*, 82.

> *So then, as we have opportunity, let us do good to everyone, and especially to those who are of the household of faith.*
> —Galatians 6:10

Before we look at our neighbours, including government and those who don't share our faith, in the next chapter let's think a little more about our brothers and sisters who are suffering for their faith in Christ. How might we engage meaningfully in Christian life and citizenship with our spiritual siblings in ways that demonstrate our love for one another, by which, Jesus said, the world may know that *we* are His disciples?

> *For through him we both have access in one Spirit to the Father. So then you are no longer strangers and aliens [sojourners], but you are fellow citizens with the saints and members of the household of God...*
> —Ephesians 2:18–19

Three Takeaways

- The Church, also called the Body of Christ, is bigger than your congregation, denomination, and all the denominations in the nation.
- From the beginning, the Body of Christ has shown capacity for the variety of expressions, languages, races, and styles Christ-followers exhibit in the global Church.
- Christians are called by Jesus to love and minister to the needs of other Christians.

CHAPTER FIVE

ONE BODY, WHEN ONE PART SUFFERS

For just as the body is one and has many members, and all the members of the body, though many, are one body, so it is with Christ. For in one Spirit we were all baptized into one body—Jews or Greeks, slaves or free—and all were made to drink of one Spirit.
—1 Corinthians 12:12–13

Let brotherly love continue. Do not neglect to show hospitality to strangers, for thereby some have entertained angels unawares. Remember those who are in prison, as though in prison with them, and those who are mistreated, since you also are in the body.
—Hebrews 13:1–3

So Peter was kept in prison, but earnest prayer for him was made to God by the church.
—Acts 12:5

ACHIEVEMENTS ARE OFTEN REWARDED WITH GIFTS. SOMETIMES WE'RE ASKED what we would like to receive. I received some great gifts when I was called to the bar of Ontario in 1990.[78] My boss let me pick out a new Bible, so I picked *The Wesley Bible*,[79] a study Bible in the New King James

---

[78] *Called to the bar* being the term used to recognize that one has completed the requirements to be a barrister and solicitor, i.e. a lawyer.

[79] *The Wesley Bible: A Personal Study Bible for Holy Living* (Nashville, TN: Thomas Nelson Publishers, 1990).

Version. My mum, after checking with us to make sure we would accept it, gifted Gloria and me with a trip to Barbados, the country of her birth and land of my heritage, cousins, aunts, and uncles.

In addition to spending a great time with family, I was captivated with the church buildings in Barbados, even spending a little cash on a book of photographs called *Historic Churches of Barbados*.[80] I didn't have a digital camera in those days, so the book was both a souvenir and film-saver.

Church buildings still hold a certain fascination for me. Riding motorcycle in North America has meant seeing a wide variety of construction styles for churches. In small-town Canada and U.S.A., we found that the best food was usually procured where the locals went to eat, which was most often across the street or within easy walking distance of a main street church building. In the big cities, older church buildings tend to be in the downtown, and they're not always used for church anymore. Contemporary church buildings are found in the suburbs, sometimes at a driving or transit distance from the homes of members, let alone a good place to find a meal.

When privileged to visit other countries, I have enjoyed viewing and visiting the locations where congregations gather for worship.

In Kenya, we worshipped in a low-ceilinged corrugated tin-roofed building with concrete block walls and open-air windows. In China, the registered church we worshipped in rivalled any architecturally modern Anglican cathedral, massive in size, beautiful in appearance, and featuring state-of-the-art electronics. Friends have worshipped in open fields with unregistered congregations in the same nation. The Cave Church in Egypt has nearly seventy thousand people in attendance weekly.[81] I hope to get there some day. In the north of Nigeria, I was privileged to address more than one hundred pastors and pastors' widows in a building that a few short weeks later would succumb to an explosion at the hands of Boko Haram militants.

---

80   Barbara Hill, *Historic Churches of Barbados* (Bridgetown, Barbados: Art Heritage Publications, 1984).
81   Dean Smith, "Egyptian Cave Church Has 70,000 People Attending Services Every Week," *Open the Word*. July 5, 2016 (https://opentheword.org/2016/07/05/egyptian-cave-church-has-70000–people-attending-services-every-week).

While the Church has inspired building styles, and most often meets for worship in buildings, it's good to know that the buildings are not the Church. Whether worshipping in a field, warehouse, cave, or cathedral, the Church is the people linked through a shared commitment to Jesus Christ, God our Father, and the ever-present Holy Spirit.

These words are being written just days after the fire at Notre Dame Cathedral in Paris, France. The image that comes to mind when I think of all that appeared in the news coverage is not so much the flames on the roof, or even the collapse of its spire, but the people gathered in the nearby streets praying, singing *Ave Maria* and other hymns from memory, at the very heart of a declared secularist nation.[82]

The first-century Church did not have buildings. Christians might have met in synagogues (until they were found out, then thrown out), in fields and open spaces, or in private residences, but they didn't flock to a church building with a sign out front for 11:00 a.m. service on Sunday morning. While many of the world's nearly two and a half billion Christians have a reasonable expectation of freedom to worship, and also to publicly promote activities at a church building, a substantial number of others face restrictions or prohibitions on assembly.

Like Saul headed for Damascus in the first century, there are in the twenty-first century many who are authorized by government, or simply permitted without obstruction by government, to persecute Christians.

In *Under Siege*, I wrote,

> In his 1997 book *Their Blood Cries Out: The Worldwide Tragedy of Modern Christians Who Are Dying for Their Faith*[83]—a book still considered by many to be the best primer for understanding the persecution of members of the global Church—Canadian Paul Marshall notes his use of the term persecution to be "the denial of any of the rights of religious freedom."[84] Marshall

---

82 Jessica Vomiero, "As Notre Dame Burned, Parisians Gathered Outside Sang 'Ave Maria'," *Global News*. April 16, 2019 (https://globalnews.ca/news/5172175/notre-dame-crowds-ave-maria).

83 Paul Marshall, *Their Blood Cries Out: The Worldwide Tragedy of Modern Christians Who Are Dying for Their Faith* (Dallas, TX: Word Publishing, 1997).

84 Ibid., 248.

uses the word denial in its strictest sense, a refusal, rejection, and disavowal of any rights of religious freedom. *Their Blood Cries Out* is a stunning introduction to the stresses, strains, and horrors being faced by Christians in nearly a third of the world's countries, and the appalling lack of interest shown by too many in the Western world.[85]

Marshall's comments have been verified statistically by Open Doors International. Open Doors describes itself as "[t]he world's largest outreach to persecuted Christians in the most high-risk places."[86] For almost thirty years,[87] benefiting from an international network of contacts, Open Doors has produced the annual World Watch List (WWL) to map and comment on the fifty most dangerous countries in the world to live as a Christian. To get its data, Open Doors uses a comprehensive nation-by-nation questionnaire completed by country specialists, often resident within the country or region, and a scoring system "that measures the degree of freedom Christians have in five key areas of life—private, family, community, national and church life. These are then added to the amount of violence they experience to provide a final score."[88] The 2019 WWL reports on 2018. It describes eleven countries where there was extreme levels of persecution, twenty-nine countries with very high levels of persecution, and ten countries with high levels of persecution. The data collection methodology is endorsed by, and the list independently audited by, the International Institute for Religious Freedom.[89]

---

85   Hutchinson, *Under Siege*, 189.
86   *Open Doors International*. Date of access: April 20, 2019 (www.opendoors.org).
87   Open Doors, *2019 World Watch List: A Guide to Global Persecution* (Halton Hills, ON: Open Doors Canada, 2019), 3.
88   Ibid., 4.
89   "The 'International Institute for Religious Freedom' (IIRF) is a network of professors, researchers, academics, specialists and university institutions from all continents which work on reliable data on the violation of religious freedom worldwide and want to implement this topic to college and university programmes and curricula, especially in the areas of law, sociology, religious studies and theological programmes" (*International Institute for Religious Freedom*. Date of access: May 30, 2019 [https://www.iirf.eu]).

More than 245 million Christians, most living in seventy-three of the world's 195 countries, experienced these three categories of persecution.[90] That's more than one of every ten Christians. More than 1,450 church and Christian buildings suffered attack, more than 3,127 Christians were detained or imprisoned without trial, and at least 4,283 Christians were verified as having been martyred, killed for their faith.[91]

In a separate document called *2019 World Watch List Report: The Rise of Religious Persecution Across the World*, Matthew Rees of Open Doors UK & Ireland describes how "the range of vulnerabilities such as gender [sexual violence against women], age [children in particular], class and ethnicity are intersecting with religious identity to create a toxic cocktail of widespread persecution."[92]

The persecution list is headed by nations with governments ideologically opposed to religion or giving preferential recognition to only one religious community, such as Buddhism, Hinduism, or one of the expressions of Islam. China moved from forty-third on the list in 2018 to twenty-seventh in 2019. Russia entered the top fifty as tension increased there for Christians who are not part of the Russian Orthodox Church as well as Christians in the Caucasus region, which is dominated by Islamic groups. India, the world's largest democracy, entered the top ten as radical Hindu groups have gained increasing influence. In Iran, another top ten country, Christianity is considered a Western influence and a threat to Islam. Nigeria had the highest verified number of Christians killed for their faith of any country in the world in 2018, more than 3,700. North Korea, where the only permissible worship is worship of Supreme Leader Kim Jong-un, retained the number one ranking it has held since 2002.

On Easter Sunday 2019 in Sri Lanka, three churches, and in Colombo some neighbouring hotels, were bombed by Muslim extremists. Christians make up less than eight percent of the population in this nation, which is ranked the forty-sixth most dangerous in the world for

---

90 Matthew Rees, *2019 World Watch List Report: The Rise of Religious Persecution Across the World* (Halton Hills, ON: Open Doors Canada, 2019), 4.
91 Open Doors, *2019 World Watch List: A Guide to Global Persecution*, 4.
92 Rees, *2019 World Watch List Report: The Rise of Religious Persecution Across the World*, 4.

Christians on the 2019 World Watch List. More than two hundred fifty were killed and five hundred injured in the Easter attacks.[93]

Christmas and Easter celebrations are particularly targeted in several countries, since many take the risk of assembly on these occasions who otherwise wouldn't attend a predictable meeting of the Church. The large gatherings of Christians present well-publicized prey and are harder to secure. The intent of the antagonists is to dissuade the Church from faith in the birth, death and resurrection of Jesus, and discourage the believers' trust in their fellow human beings.

On Palm Sunday 2017, suicide bombers killed forty-four people in two Coptic churches in Egypt.[94] Also in 2017, suicide bombers killed nine and wounded fifty-six the Sunday before Christmas at a Methodist Church in Quetta, Pakistan, although it was being guarded by police.[95] Even a "safe" country like the United States is not immune. In Portland, Oregon an SUV was deliberately driven into a Vietnamese Catholic Church on Christmas Eve.[96]

Another international ministry that specializes in working with the global Church experiencing persecution is The Voice of the Martyrs. The Voice of the Martyrs' international network is known as the International Christian Association, and it goes by a variety of names in different countries, including: The Voice of the Martyrs, Voice of the

---

[93] Kate Shellnut, "Easter Bombings Kill 290 at Sri Lankan Churches and Hotels," *Christianity Today*. April 21, 2019 (https://www.christianitytoday.com/news/2019/april/easter-church-bombings-kill-200–in-sri-lanka.html). See also: Jayson Casper, "Sri Lankan Sunday School Was 'Willing to Die for Christ' on Easter. Half Did," *Christianity Today*. April 25, 2019 (https://www.christianitytoday.com/news/2019/april/sri-lanka-easter-isis-zion-sunday-school-sebastian-funerals.html).

[94] Magdy Samaan and Declan Walsh, "Egypt Declares State of Emergency, as Attacks Undercut Promise of Security," *New York Times*. April 9, 2017 (https://www.nytimes.com/2017/04/09/world/middleeast/explosion-egypt-coptic-christian-church.html).

[95] Gul Yousafzai and Asif Shahzad, "Suicide Bombers Attack Church in Pakistan's Quetta Before Christmas, Killing Nine," *Reuters*. December 17, 2017 (https://www.reuters.com/article/us-pakistan-attack/suicide-bombers-attack-church-in-pakistans-quetta-before-christmas-killing-nine-idUSKBN1EB08E).

[96] Catholic News Service, "Vietnamese Parishioners Don't Let Attack on Church Deter Christmas," *Crux*. December 26, 2018 (https://cruxnow.com/church-in-the-usa/2018/12/26/vietnamese-parishioners-dont-let-attack-on-church-deter-christmas).

Christian Martyrs, Release International, and Christian Mission International. This network serves persecuted and struggling Christians in a number of ways, connecting Christians who have freedom with those whose freedom is restricted.

One theme The Voice of the Martyrs has focused on is telling anecdotal stories from the Church in distant lands to the part of the Body that has abundant religious freedom. These true stories inform and equip us to pray for, encourage, and support our brothers and sisters in Christ who are reviled, persecuted, and have all kinds of evil uttered against them falsely on account of their faithfulness to Jesus (Matthew 5:11).

The Voice of the Martyrs Canada has a bookmark that succinctly describes a "persecution scale," explained using Scripture:

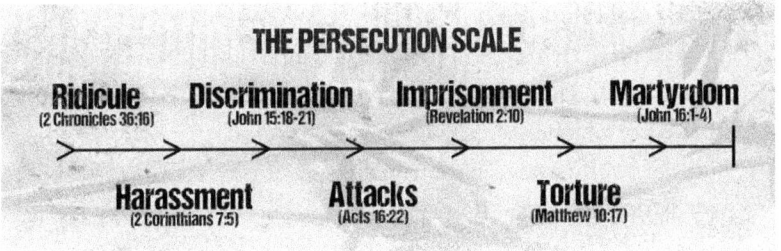

The Voice of the Martyrs Canada, Persecution Scale Bookmark.
I encourage you to look up the Scripture references

In *Under Siege*, I outlined five commonly referenced stages of persecution. You will notice that the five stages align with The Voice of the Martyrs' seven-point persecution scale.

> The first stage is stereotyping the group. Generalizing a quality that describes a whole group is stereotyping. ...
>
> The second stage is vilification. This is the word the Supreme Court of Canada used as the point of definition for hate speech in its 2013 decision in *Saskatchewan (Human Rights Commission) v. Whatcott*:[97]

---

97 *Saskatchewan (Human Rights Commission) v. Whatcott*, 2013 SCC 11, [2013] 1 SCR 467. For a brief case description, see Judicial Sources in this book's bibliography.

> 41. …Representations vilifying a person or group will seek to abuse, denigrate or delegitimize them, to render them lawless, dangerous, unworthy or unacceptable in the eyes of the audience. Expression exposing vulnerable groups to detestation and vilification goes far beyond merely discrediting, humiliating or offending the victims.

The third stage is marginalization. Once it has been determined that the general characteristic (stereotype) of an individual or group is bad, and they are unworthy of general acceptance (vilification), the next step is to make them unwelcome. Treating others as insignificant and outside the scope of acceptability delegitimizes their participation in societal dialogue.

The fourth stage is the one at which official state action is required. The individual or group is criminalized for their beliefs or practices…

The fifth stage is outright persecution. This may take place through social hostility, not officially sponsored by the state but often sanctioned by the state, or political hostility that is endorsed by state officials (e.g. people are beaten by neighbours simply because of their religious beliefs and the state takes no restrictive or punitive action with the neighbours, or perhaps the state authorizes such action if someone speaks publicly about a minority faith belief).

Stages four and five are the stages where the risk of death becomes a present reality.[98]

Canadian Glenn Penner, the late CEO of Voice of the Martyrs Canada, in his book *In the Shadow of the Cross: A Biblical Theology of Persecution and Discipleship*,[99] outlines quick lessons for the twenty-first-century

---

98 Hutchinson, *Under Siege*, 190–191.
99 Glenn Penner, *In the Shadow of the Cross: A Biblical Theology of Persecution and Discipleship* (Bartlesville, OK: Living Sacrifice Books, 2004).

Church. These are challenges for us today from the responses of the seven first-century churches described in the Book of Revelation:

> *When faced with persecution, some churches, like the one in Ephesus, in their zeal to defend the faith, become bastions of strict, unloving orthodoxy (2:1–7). Others, like the church in Smyrna, need to be encouraged not to give in to fear in the face of suffering (2:8–11). The scourge of false doctrine creeping in from the outside endangers some faithful churches, like the one in Pergamum (2:12–17). Yet others, like in Thyatira, struggle to maintain ethical and moral purity, especially when the culture demands compromise in order to continue to make a living (2:18–29). The church in Sardis illustrates that persecuted Christians are not immune from spiritual deadness (3:1–6), while some churches, as in Philadelphia, need to be encouraged to look beyond their own neediness to the opportunities that God has placed before them (3:7–13). The Laodicean church might well represent the church that, like in Corinth, forgets that this world is not all there is. Such churches deal with opposition by assimilation into the culture and adopting the trappings of success. They forget that the time to sit on thrones is in the future (3:21) and not today. The task of Christ's Church is to carry the cross in the pursuit of the goals of the kingdom of God. By pursuing the goals of this world, the Laodiceans may have removed the offense of the cross, but they had incurred the offense of Christ.* [100]

Christians weren't perfect in the first century. We're still not perfect in the twenty-first. I wrote,

> …Jesus' words to John for the seven churches were about faithfulness, not perfection. When signs of persecution become evident, at whatever stage, it is crucial that we, the Church, look to Jesus. The promises found in John's letter for those who overcome persecution through faithfulness to Jesus are wonderful. As my pastor Jason Boucher says, "God isn't just good. He's amazing!"

---

[100] Penner, *In the Shadow of the Cross*, 252.

When we hear stories of persecution, especially living in a social media world where tweets, posts, and blogs are often circulated with a single click, we have an obligation to do our best to verify the truth of the story before we pass it along. Often we can do that by only sharing from sources that have developed a good reputation for truth. Other times, we can verify stories by means of a simple internet search.[101]

When we receive or pass along reports of persecution, let us be mindful that continuing to faithfully live for Christ is a challenge for many Christ-followers in other nations, and a daily achievement. When asked what their brothers and sisters with greater freedom might do for them, the most often heard response is the simple request to remember them as if we are with them, and pray that they would remain faithful.

Remember, in the Body of Christ, *they* are *us*.

Taking a lesson from the first century, in addition to answering the request for remembrance and prayer, let us provide other practical support to our brothers and sisters in Christ. Perhaps a most effective way to do so would be through trustworthy emissaries, like Paul on his way to Jerusalem (Romans 15:25–26; 1 Corinthians 16:1–4; 2 Corinthians 8:1–5; Galatians 2:10). In practical terms, this may mean building trustworthy relationships within the Church, across the street, across oceans, or across continents, supporting ministries working with the persecuted, or perhaps sponsoring Christian refugees, among other opportunities.

Three Takeaways

- The Church is people, not buildings.
- Christians in dozens of nations worldwide live with persecution, including threats of violence and death, simply because they are Christian.
- Remember our brothers and sisters in Christ who are suffering, pray for them, and explore the opportunities to provide them with other practical support.

---

101 Hutchinson, *Under Siege*, 192–193.

CHAPTER SIX

CHRISTIANS, DUAL CITIZENS IN THE WORLD

I do not ask that you take them out of the world, but that you keep them from the evil one.

—John 17:15

But our citizenship is in heaven...

—Philippians 3:20

WHEN MY PARENTS AND SISTERS FIRST CAME TO CANADA, THEY WERE CITIZENS of Barbados. Even after becoming Canadian citizens, traces of the Bajan accent lingered.

Dad loved the ocean. He left it behind to pursue a different, hopefully better future for his children. But love of the ocean endured deep in his being. Before journeying heavenward, Dad asked that his ashes be scattered in the surf of Barbados. Although resident in one place, his heart citizenship was held by another. The songs he requested for his funeral reflected enduring love for his beautiful Barbados and his hope-filled anticipation of heaven.

My uncle Geoff also had the music of Barbados played at his funeral. He had followed his stepbrother, my dad, to Canada. During the funeral, the priest shared the following story. Living in Barbados, with plans to move to Canada, created a measure of excitement about the future. At the airport, it was difficult to leave friends and family. At the next airport, it was exhilarating to be greeted by waiting friends and family! Comparing the experience to departure from this world and arrival in heaven, I was reminded that as Christians we are dual citizens; one citizenship is here on Earth, whatever country we hold dear, and the other citizenship is in heaven. As dual citizens, we hold both at the same time but live only in one place at a time.

It is an almost unfathomable mystery that God formulated His plan of redemption for as-yet-unformed, soon-to-be-sinful humankind before the foundation of the world. The plan that would rest on His own brief time as a dual citizen on Earth, from a baby whose yet-to-be-born cousin leapt in the womb at His foetal presence (Luke 1:41) until His publicly documented crucifixion in Jerusalem little more than three decades after His relatively obscure birth in nearby Bethlehem.

It's a great mystery that *"all who did receive him [Jesus, God the Son], who believed in his name, he gave the right to become children of God [the Father]"* (John 1:12), citizens first of Earth and then of the eternal heaven even while continuing to live in this world. It's another mystery that, after believing in His name, it takes time for us to be *"conformed to the image of his Son, in order that he might be the firstborn among many brothers"* (Romans 8:29).

The Body of Christ is one big, imperfect perfect family. That's what it is to live as Christians. We are perfectly and wholly children of God. We are, at the same time, imperfect human beings. We are citizens of heaven, whose citizenship is being more fully formed while we remain citizens in this world.

The context of the Church is both an everlasting relationship with God—Father, Son, and Holy Spirit—and the temporal world in which we live.

The other important part of our context is the one in which the New Testament, an enduring and vital instruction to the Church, was written. That context was first-century Judaism within the Roman Empire, beginning at the heart of Judaism in Jerusalem. Remember, non-Jewish observers and the first generation of Christ-followers regarded Christianity as an expression of Judaism, which included the heritage linked to the sacred text Christians now refer to as the Old Testament. Thus, the Church found itself located at the intersection of citizenship in this world, citizenship in heaven, and Judaism.

American New Testament scholar Marcus J. Borg wrote,

First-century Judaism was diverse. In the Jewish homeland, there were a number of groups with different ways of being Jewish within the context of Roman rule, which began in 63 BCE, about sixty years before Jesus was born.[102]

Borg describes four identifiable communities that had a public profile, and he also notes that a number of Jews did not belong to any of the four. The Essenes withdrew from the mainstream and lived what we would now call a monastic lifestyle. Zealots opposed the Romans and sought some means to forcibly overthrow their presence. The Sadducees were a wealthier class who opted to cooperate, even collaborate, with the Romans. The Pharisees undertook to live a religious lifestyle within society, one that would demonstrably distinguish them from non-Jews.[103]

It's not hard to see how this array has carried forward into Christianity. We, too, may desire to enter a monastic life. Political engagement may result in strategizing to defeat a government (although, hopefully not by force) or to cooperate with the government, either generally or on select issues. For me, there is an admirable quality to those Christians who seek to live in a way that is evidently Christ-following and discernibly different from those around us.

Borg identified a set of core beliefs considered key to this variety of expressions: the *Shema Yisrael* (Deuteronomy 6:4), God's covenant with Abraham that promised them the land and a theology that provided for practical application of religious beliefs to daily life.[104]

It's hardly surprising that Christians, too, accept the truth that there is only one God. Although most of us are not in the genealogical lineage, we consider ourselves to be spiritual children of Abraham (Romans 4:16–25; Galatians 3:7–9, 14–18, 29). And a refrain heard throughout the New Testament is that our religious beliefs have practical application to daily life, sometimes guiding us into alignment with the culture around us, and sometimes markedly setting us apart from the values of that culture.

---

102 Borg, *Evolution of the Word*, 7.
103 Ibid.
104 Borg, *Evolution of the Word*, 7–8.

PART I: CHURCH

Jesus of Nazareth, whom we call Christ, was Jewish. He did not personally write a single word of the New Testament. Yet He inspired every one.

If Jesus did write anything, we don't have a copy of it. What we have is an historic record of Jesus speaking. In the rabbinical tradition, He spoke to explain the written Word (Old Testament), illustrate the truths of the kingdom of heaven, and present the practical application of His teaching for everyday life.

The New Testament is also a record of Christian leaders, influenced by the Holy Spirit, giving written guidance to other Christ-followers.

Even though this took place in the interactive context of first-century Judaism within the Roman Empire, the eternal nature of its truth continues to speak to us today.

At whatever point in life one's earthly citizenship intersects with one's heavenly citizenship, the intent is that both be lived out where we are. You've likely heard the saying that a person is "too heavenly minded to be any earthly good." The promise of heaven is not about escaping the realities of daily life, but living them with a different worldview, an inspired perspective, a certain faith, and an outlook informed by eternal truth and awareness of eternal destiny.

Paul wrote about the tension of living with dual citizenship, both earthly and heavenly:

> *For we know that if the tent that is our earthly home is destroyed, we have a building from God, a house not made with hands, eternal in the heavens. For in this tent we groan, longing to put on our heavenly dwelling… So we are always of good courage. We know that while we are at home in the body we are away from the Lord, for we walk by faith, not by sight. Yes, we are of good courage, and we would rather be away from the body and at home with the Lord. So whether we are at home or away, we make it our aim to please him.*
> —2 Corinthians 5:1–2, 6–9

> *…as always Christ will be honored in my body, whether by life or by death. For to me to live is Christ, and to die is gain. If I am to live in the*

flesh, that means fruitful labor for me. Yet which I shall choose I cannot tell. I am hard pressed between the two. My desire is to depart and be with Christ, for that is far better. But to remain in the flesh is more necessary on your account. Convinced of this, I know that I will remain and continue with you all, for your progress and joy in the faith, so that in me you may have ample cause to glory in Christ Jesus, because of my coming to you again.

Only let your manner of life be worthy of the gospel of Christ...
—Philippians 1:20–27

Paul's words illuminate our understanding that, for the Christian, the appeal of heaven is balanced with the importance of living a life on Earth that witnesses to who Jesus is for us today, and who we are for Him.

In January 1983, Gloria and I set out in our 1969 Volkswagen Beetle for an epic winter road trip from Toronto, Ontario to Prince Rupert on the north coast of British Columbia. We were headed to Port Simpson (*Lax Kw'alaams*) to lead our first congregation together.

Along the way, we stopped for a few days to visit with friends in Calgary before turning north. That Sunday, we shared some time with our friends Dave and Joann and another Salvation Army pastor couple who were visiting, Lindsay and Lynette Rowe. That evening at church, Lynette sang one of her original compositions for us, "He Didn't Say that It Would Be Easy":

He didn't say that it would be easy,
To bear His cross of shame,
He didn't say that it would be easy,
To follow in His name.
But He said, "My Grace all sufficient will help you through each day,"
He didn't say that it would be easy,
But He'll be there every step of the way,
Yes, He'll be there every step of the way.

> He didn't say that it would be easy,
> To leave your home that's here,
> And to follow wherever He leads you,
> To go with Him anywhere,
> But He said, "As I was with Moses, So I will be with you,"
> He didn't say that it would be easy,
> But His grace will surely see you through,
> Don't you know that He's depending on you?
>
> He didn't say that it would be easy,
> To lead men to His throne,
> Even He was despised and rejected,
> Yes, He suffered all alone,
> But He said, "Now go preach My Gospel,
> And show them I'm the way,"
> Your reward will be given in Glory,
> For He's coming to take us away,
> Yes, He's coming for us any day.[105]

Lynette gave me a copy of the lyrics, which I kept in the flyleaf of my Bible and reflected on frequently. The melody, or at least the version of it stuck in my head, remained with me over the decades. Even after that Bible was stolen and the contents of the flyleaf long lost, this song offered inspiration—a reminder of our dual citizenship and Jesus' presence with us in the here and now.

In his closing words to those first disciples, Jesus committed to be with His followers *always* (Matthew 28:20), through all of life on earth and then in heaven. But first, as dinner on the evening of His betrayal came to an end, He prayed to His Father, our Father, for those in the upper room with Him, and for us. Here's a portion of that prayer:

> *But now I am coming to you, and these things I speak in the world, that they may have my joy fulfilled in themselves. I have given them your word, and the world has hated them because they are not of the world,*

---

105 Lynette Rowe, "He Didn't Say that It Would Be Easy," 1981. Used with permission.

CHRISTIANS, DUAL CITIZENS IN THE WORLD

> *just as I am not of the world. I do not ask that you take them out of the world, but that you keep them from the evil one. They are not of the world, just as I am not of the world. Sanctify them in the truth; your word is truth. As you sent me into the world, so I have sent them into the world. And for their sake I consecrate myself, that they also may be sanctified in truth.*
>
> *I do not ask for these only, but also for those who will believe in me through their word, that they may all be one, just as you, Father, are in me, and I in you, that they also may be in us, so that the world may believe that you have sent me.*
>
> —John 17:13–21

Let's reflect for a moment on the alternate translation for the word *sanctify* in the above passage, "set apart for holy service.":

> *[Set them apart for holy service] in the truth; your word is truth. As you sent me into the world, so I have sent them into the world. And for their sake I [set myself apart for holy service], that they also may be [set apart for holy service] in truth.*
>
> *I do not ask for these only, but also for those who will believe in me through their word...*
>
> —John 17:17–20

Jesus didn't say it would be easy for us. It wasn't easy for Him. It wasn't easy for Paul.

The following chapters will give fuller consideration to what it means to live life set apart for holy service as heaven's citizens, set apart for Him and sent to live as His witnesses (Acts 1:8) and ambassadors (2 Corinthians 5:20), as earthly citizens in the world of the twenty-first century.

As you read on, bear in mind the dual citizenship we hold in heaven and on earth, observing the nature of your heavenly citizenship and considering the distinctives of your national citizenship.

PART I: CHURCH

Three Takeaways

- Heavenly citizenship does not excuse us from engaging in earthly citizenship.
- Our heavenly citizenship informs our participation in earthly citizenship.
- Exercising earthly citizenship in a God-honouring way is part of our Christian witness.

PART II:
IN SOCIETY

But understand this, that in the last days there will come times of difficulty. For people will be lovers of self, lovers of money, proud, arrogant, abusive, disobedient to their parents, ungrateful, unholy, heartless, unappeasable, slanderous, without self-control, brutal, not loving good, treacherous, reckless, swollen with conceit, lovers of pleasure rather than lovers of God, having the appearance of godliness, but denying its power. Avoid such people.

—2 Timothy 3:1–5

Be subject for the Lord's sake to every human institution, whether it be to the emperor as supreme, or to governors as sent by him to punish those who do evil and to praise those who do good. For this is the will of God, that by doing good you should put to silence the ignorance of foolish people. Live as people who are free, not using your freedom as a cover-up for evil, but living as servants of God. Honor everyone. Love the brotherhood. Fear God. Honor the emperor.

—1 Peter 2:13–17

Put not your trust in princes, in a son of man, in whom there is no salvation. When his breath departs, he returns to the earth; on that very day his plans perish. Blessed is he whose help is the God of Jacob, whose hope is in the Lord his God, who made heaven and earth, the sea, and all that is in them, who keeps faith forever.

—Psalm 146:3–6

Therefore render to Caesar the things that are Caesar's, and to God the things that are God's.

—Matthew 22:21

CHAPTER SEVEN

THE CHURCH, CITIZENS IN THE NATION

> *Thus says the Lord of hosts, the God of Israel, to all the exiles whom I have sent into exile from Jerusalem to Babylon: Build houses and live in them; plant gardens and eat their produce. Take wives and have sons and daughters; take wives for your sons, and give your daughters in marriage, that they may bear sons and daughters; multiply there, and do not decrease. But seek the welfare of the city where I have sent you into exile, and pray to the Lord on its behalf, for in its welfare you will find your welfare.*
>
> —Jeremiah 29:4–7

WE EACH LIVE AS A CITIZEN OF A NATION, WITH THE ATTENDANT RIGHTS, responsibilities, and risks of that citizenship. While some countries allow for dual citizenship, God expects it. Paul reminds us that we are citizens of heaven (Philippians 3:20) and ambassadors of heaven's King (2 Corinthians 5:20). Throughout the Bible, we find reflection on that dual citizenship, including principles relating to the practical implications for our earthly interests and behaviour.

Both citizenships are carried out not only as individuals, but in the context of community. The concepts that follow are necessarily for the individual Christian and for the collective Church. Canadian pastor and educator George M. Tuttle noted,

> Just as the individual person cannot exist apart from society, so the individual Christian is part of a larger body, the body

of Christ or the Church. We must expect therefore that Christian social action is encumbent [sic] not only upon individual Christians but upon the Church as a whole.[106]

Gloria and I have been privileged to consistently be members in congregations and denominations that take seriously both the *love one another* commandment and the *love your neighbour as yourself* commandment.[107]

In addition to Sunday services, Sunday school, youth groups, and home groups, the congregation we joined shortly after we moved to Ottawa has a Bible school, attended by people from several congregations, and a community food bank, among other ministries. Ten percent of our congregational revenue is given to other Christian ministries that work locally, nationally, and globally for the Church and for the community outside the Church. Benevolent support is also available to families and individuals in the congregation who find themselves in need. We've done some out of the ordinary things that send the message that we love one another, such as one time giving a single mom a car, as well as fun and supportive activities that let the community know we care about more than just ourselves. An example of this is our annual community funfair, featuring free haircuts and backpack-with-school-supplies giveaway, in a neighbourhood where parents appreciate the easing of some financial burdens and an enjoyable day with their children. Our food cupboard is in the same neighbourhood.

We're not a perfect church. We are a healthy church, actively loving God, loving one another, and loving our neighbours while continuing to learn and grow in our love for God, one another, and our neighbours.

Loving one another within the Church doesn't take away from our call or capacity to love our neighbours. It's a precursor to doing so well. Understanding and practising how to love ourselves within the Church is, as Jesus said, the example by which *"all people will know that you are my disciples"* (John 13:35). Loving one another also empowers us to love our neighbours as ourselves (Mark 12:31). Having learned to identify

---

[106] George M. Tuttle, *The Christian as Citizen* (Canada: Publications Committee, Department of Education, Canadian Council of Churches, 1949), 27.
[107] And, yes, the *love the Lord your God* commandment comes first!

and meet needs within the Body of Christ, we are better equipped to recognize and respond to the needs of neighbours who might not share our faith.

Before we look at our rights as citizens, let's consider some foundational thoughts on the responsibilities connected with loving our neighbours. Like Paul in the first century, our rights as Christians in the twenty-first century are either invoked or set aside because we understand our responsibilities under God and His Word, including the importance of advancing His message.

Paul would have understood the importance of the Jewish concept of *shalom*. While he had much to say on this topic, Paul summarized *shalom* in a short sentence in one of his letters to persecuted Christians of the first century: *"If possible, so far as it depends on you, live peaceably with all"* (Romans 12:18). From that place of peace, Paul, as well as other New Testament authors, challenges us, as part of our Christian witness, to contribute to the society in which we live, whether that society be receptive or hostile to our efforts for the common good.

In *"the letter that Jeremiah the prophet sent from Jerusalem to the surviving elders of the exiles, and to the priests, the prophets, and all the people, whom Nebuchadnezzar had taken into exile from Jerusalem to Babylon,"* (Jeremiah 29:1) God, through Jeremiah, addressed the situation in an environment hostile to Judaism by encouraging the Jews to live life in as typical a way as they could, and challenged the people to contribute to *"the welfare of the city where I have sent you into exile, and pray to the Lord on its behalf, for in its welfare you will find your welfare"* (Jeremiah 29:7).

John Stackhouse, a Canadian academic and practical theologian recognized for his work on the interaction between Church and culture, summed up the idea this way:

> We are not to simply observe the world, nor even merely to enjoy it. We are to make something of it. That's what *culture* is. The world is a giant studio, filled with paints and canvases and brushes and easels into which God invites the human beings as artists. The world is very good, yes, but it is *wild*—and

therefore needs to be subdued, to be ruled, to be cultivated so that it becomes everything that it can be.

This idea that everything is to become all it can be is the heart of the Hebrew word *shalom*. Usually translated "peace," *shalom* means not only something negative—"no war or conflict of any kind"—but also something wonderfully positive: the *flourishing* of all things. This flourishing is not only of each individual thing—each human being, yes, and also each animal, tree, landscape, and waterway—but also of each *relationship* among individuals, each *group* that individuals form, each *relationship* among groups or between groups and individuals, and the whole of creation in loving harmony with God. *Shalom* is literally *global flourishing*, and it is the intended outcome of God working with God's "little gods" to cultivate the world.[108]

Our citizenship in heaven compels us to be good citizens—contributors to society, culture, and the well-being of all creation—through the means of our participatory citizenship here on Earth. Our contribution is to be secured by a motivation of Christian love, personal humility, and the desire to "work for those policies which express God's will in our time."[109]

Jesus expressed this three-part challenge for our engagement with both Church and neighbours by way of clear instruction, including admonition to influence and lead through service.

> *And Jesus called them to him and said to them, "You know that those who are considered rulers of the Gentiles lord it over them, and their*

---

[108] John G. Stackhouse, Jr., *Why You're Here: Ethics for the Real World* (New York, NY: Oxford University Press, 2018), 18.

[109] Tuttle, *Christian as Citizen*, 24. In pages 22–25, Tuttle covers three points concerning our motivation, our humility, and God's will. Tuttle notes, "In conformity with this principle historical understanding of the Bible persuaded us that much of the counsel on social questions offered by the prophets and Jesus and Paul was conditioned by the prevailing world-view of their time and the current social situation. While the principles laid down are binding for all ages, applications of these principles are determined by local circumstances… We don't need a new set of moral principles. We need only to apply the teachings of Jesus and of Paul to a world situation which is very different from anything they experienced" (24–25).

> *great ones exercise authority over them. But it shall not be so among you. But whoever would be great among you must be your servant [dia-konos, one who ministers in service to another, attends to the needs of another*[110]*], and whoever would be first among you must be slave [dou-los, one who gives oneself over in subservience to another*[111]*] of all."*
>
> —Mark 10:42–44

In the previous chapter, we considered the perspective of *love one another* in reference to Jesus' words in Matthew 25:40: *"Truly, I say to you, as you did it to one of the least of these my brothers [and sisters], you did to me."* Such consideration doesn't inevitably limit the meaning of our doing *"for the least of these"* to doing something for the Church. Within the Church, we might do well to ask ourselves, what if the perspective on the verses that follow in that discourse are a reference to our neighbours?

> *"Then he will say to those on his left, "Depart from me, you cursed, into the eternal fire prepared for the devil and his angels. For I was hungry and you gave me no food, I was thirsty and you gave me no drink, I was a stranger and you did not welcome me, naked and you did not clothe me, sick and in prison and you did not visit me."*
>
> *Then they also will answer, saying, "Lord, when did we see you hungry or thirsty or a stranger or naked or sick or in prison, and did not minister to you?"*
>
> *Then he will answer them, saying, "Truly, I say to you, as you did not do it to one of the least of these, you did not do it to me."*
>
> —Matthew 25:41–45

Here, Jesus makes no mention of brothers and sisters but simply compassion for *"the least of these."* What if we are to care for the least of these who are our brothers and sisters in the Church in order to better prepare us to care for the least of these who are not in the Church? Or perhaps we are to do both simultaneously?

---

110 James Strong, *Strong's Exhaustive Concordance, Greek Dictionary of the New Testament*, #1249.
111 Ibid., #1401.

The greater context of these remarks (Matthew 25:31–46), made on the Mount of Olives, is Jesus' commentary beginning at Matthew 24:3 about our personal need of preparation for the end of the age and the final judgement—the division of people from all nations between those who are found righteous and those who are found wanting.

This is not to imply that our redemption depends on performing works. It is a recognition of James' inspired charge to Christians that we *"be doers of the word, and not hearers only"* (James 1:22).

> *What good is it, my brothers, if someone says he has faith but does not have works? ...faith by itself, if it does not have works, is dead... faith was active along with his works, and faith was completed by his works... For as the body apart from the spirit is dead, so also faith apart from works is dead.*
>
> —James 2:14, 17, 22, 26

The challenge to the Church remains that we must serve to meet needs within the Church and we must serve beyond ourselves. We are ambassadors for Christ in our nation, and all nations. In Psalm 24:1, we are reminded how all-encompassing are our stewardship (of God's creation as His under-stewards) and ambassadorial responsibilities:

> *The earth is the Lord's and the fullness thereof, the world and those who dwell therein...*

This encompasses all areas of life, beginning with family and church, then extending to business, education, academics, evangelism, voluntarism, charity, ecology, economy, and politics. In fact, in neighbourhoods around the world the Church has engaged in a range of *love your neighbour* activities, such as: providing medical care, education, housing, and access to fresh water; promoting economic stability through agricultural training, complete with seeds, animals, and equipment; making available business micro-loans and mentoring; emergency disaster relief; and political advocacy on a range of issues from advancing racial equality and religious freedom to pursuing the end of human trafficking.

In regard to active participation in politics, Tuttle distinguishes individual Christians from the collective Church, putting forward words of caution:

> It may be regarded as a Christian duty to take part in politics, especially where democratic procedures not only make possible but welcome practical expressions of Christian faith, what about the Church as a whole? Should the Church support some political party which appears most nearly to satisfy the demands of Christian living? There is nothing in theory to prevent such a policy, but in practice the matter is less simple.
>
> To begin with, political parties are fallible. A given party may be right on one issue and wrong on another. In committing herself on one particular issue the Church ought not to be involved in all others by virtue of a party tag… Perhaps most important of all, however, is the historical fact that the Church itself has suffered corruption when it has been aligned with any specific party and manoeuvered into a place of political power.[112]

We will examine this issue in more detail in Chapter Twelve, including consideration of when the Church may find consideration of collective public action necessary.

The compulsion to express our heavenly citizenship on Earth is expansive—*"the world and those who dwell therein"* (Psalm 24:1). As Genesis also notes, our neighbours are as much made in the image of God as you and me (Genesis 1:27). Even when not brothers and sisters in Christ, all are brothers and sisters in humanity.

Like the congregation of which I am a member, we the Church won't be perfect, but we can be loving, humble, and an influence for the expression of God's will in our time. All the while, we continue to learn and grow in our relationship with God, His Church, and our neighbours in the nation in which we live.

---

112 Tuttle, *Christian as Citizen*, 39–40.

PART II: IN SOCIETY

One lesson of history is that nations come and nations go. Some suggest that planet Earth is progressively moving toward a future in which there will be one world government. Half a century ago, in his book *Lament for a Nation*, Canadian Christian philosopher and political commentator George Grant ruminated on this proposal.

> The universal and homogeneous state is the pinnacle of political striving. "Universal" implies a world-wide state, which would eliminate the curse of war among nations; "homogeneous" means that all men would be equal, and war among classes would be eliminated. The masses and the philosophers have both agreed that this universal and egalitarian society is the goal of historical striving. It gives content to the rhetoric of both Communists and capitalists. This state will be achieved by means of modern science...[113]

But as Grant concluded,

> Beyond courage, it is possible to live in the ancient faith, which asserts that changes in the world, even if they be recognized more as a loss than a gain, take place within an eternal order that is not affected by their taking place. Whatever the difficulty of philosophy, the religious man has been told that process is not all. *"Tendebanteque manus ripae ulteriaoris amore."* [Grant footnotes the English translation: "They were holding their arms outstretched in love toward the further shore."][114]

Drawing our minds back from the distant further shore, that place where we will find *"a better country, that is, a heavenly one,"* (Hebrews 11:16), in the following chapters we will look at our earthly citizenship

---

[113] George Grant, *Lament for a Nation: The Defeat of Canadian Nationalism*, 40th Anniversary Edition (Montreal, QC: McGill-Queen's University Press, 2005), 52.
[114] Ibid., 95. Grant also footnotes the source of this quote—Virgil, *Aeneid* (Book VI).

and the influence we might have today as ambassadors for the kingdom of heaven that has been here, is here, and is not yet fully here.[115]

Exercising our rights of citizenship without regard for the responsibilities of citizenship would be unbalanced and quickly become self-centred rather than *shalom*-focused. Knowing something of our responsibilities for the common good of human flourishing, we are better prepared to consider their application in the context of national citizenship rights.

It is indispensable that Christians be intentionally upward-minded (Romans 12:2) as a manifestation of our heavenly citizenship, and invaluable that we be conscientious and forward-thinking in our earthly citizenship.

Three Takeaways

- Loving our neighbours requires *shalom* from us.
- *Shalom* requires us to be contributors for the good of the society in which we live.
- Nations are not eternal. People, including our neighbours, are.

---

115 George Eldon Ladd, *The Gospel of the Kingdom: Scriptural Studies in the Kingdom of God* (Grand Rapids, MI: Wm. B. Eerdmans Publishing Co, 2002). Ladd explains theologically that God's sovereign reign was manifest in the past, was expressed in and through Jesus Christ, and "manifests itself both in the future and in the present and thereby creates a future realm and a present realm in which men may experience the blessings of His reign," noting that "it is a clear teaching of the New Testament that God's will is not to be *perfectly* realized in this age" (24).

CHAPTER EIGHT

THE STATE, CITIZENS' RIGHTS AND RELIGION

But when they had stretched him out for the whips, Paul said to the centurion who was standing by, "Is it lawful for you to flog a man who is a Roman citizen and uncondemned?"

When the centurion heard this, he went to the tribune and said to him, "What are you about to do? For this man is a Roman citizen."

So the tribune came and said to him, "Tell me, are you a Roman citizen?"

And he said, "Yes."

The tribune answered, "I bought this citizenship for a large sum."

Paul said, "But I am a citizen by birth."

So those who were about to examine him withdrew from him immediately, and the tribune also was afraid, for he realized that Paul was a Roman citizen and that he had bound him.

—Acts 22:25–29

AS MENTIONED EARLIER, IN JUNE 2011 I TRAVELLED AS PART OF A TEAM THAT distributed food aid, provided medical assistance, and offered encouragement to Christians in northern Nigeria. Two months earlier, the area had experienced a widespread surge in anti-Christian violence following a stunning presidential election victory by Goodluck Jonathan, a Christian who had initially become president when his Muslim predecessor died in office. Jonathan served as Nigeria's third president in the nation's fourth constitutional republic, which had followed intermittent elected governments (the first three republics) and military rule after Nigeria gained independence in 1960.

When planning travel to a foreign nation, I make use of my Canadian citizenship by accessing the tools found on the Government of Canada's website under Travel and Tourism, including registration of my travel details. In my notebook for the trip, I record the contact information for Canadian embassies, both for emergency situations and to notify them if my travel plans change. The details are also added to all electronic devices that will accompany me. If travelling into a potential danger zone, I make direct contact with officials at Foreign Affairs Canada (now Global Affairs Canada) for additional advice.

Foreign Affairs gave me some extra guidance for that trip: remove visible indicia of being Canadian from my luggage, person, etc. At the time, the foreign nationals considered to be safest in Nigeria were Americans. The U.S. had a reputation for not negotiating with kidnappers or terrorists and would use military force to free captive Americans or avenge murdered Americans. In short, at that point in history it was safer to be perceived as an American than to display an unfamiliar flag to any potential troublemakers.

Arrangements for daily interaction were coordinated with a contact I made at the High Commission of Canada to Nigeria. Based on my itinerary, he let me know where the closest Canadian-friendly locations were in the event of a crisis. He even recommended a restaurant for the evening when we took our hosts out for dinner!

I took full advantage of the benefits provided by my Canadian citizenship, to the extent feasible in a foreign nation where I had no rights of citizenship.

The concept of citizenship has long been set in the framework of the nation-state. Sometimes this is referred to as *passport citizenship*, the willingness to issue a passport, an acknowledgement by the state that you belong to it (and it belongs to you), even if rights and freedoms within the nation-state may not be equally applied (or even denied) to citizens, non-citizen residents, and visitors. That's the contemporary context in which we understand our rights and freedoms, citizens of the nation in which we live. The rights associated with our citizenship are

THE STATE, CITIZENS' RIGHTS AND RELIGION

shaped by the constitution and laws of our country, and influenced by international declarations, covenants, agreements, and treaties.

From their origin, Canadian courts have looked beyond their own decisions when considering the structure of Canadian law. Historically, Canada's courts have been informed by decisions from the courts of England and Great Britain. Over time, they have been progressively influenced by decisions made elsewhere in the common-law commonwealth. In Quebec, Canada's only civil law jurisdiction, European courts have had influence. More recently, assessment of the Canadian situation is also made with reference to decisions of an increasing range of international adjudicators, including United Nations' bodies, and assessment of both binding and non-binding UN documents that have been accepted by the Government of Canada. Canadian courts have made, and increasingly make, decisions that define the rights and freedoms of Canadians with comparison to how those rights and freedoms are understood elsewhere in the world.[116]

At times, Canadian courts' interpretation of citizens' rights situate us as citizens in a uniquely Canadian context. On other occasions, there is acknowledgement of a broader, internationally shared understanding of the rights being considered. As one might expect, the decisions of Canadian courts also influence the deliberations of courts and tribunals in other parts of the globe. As the world has become metaphorically smaller—quicker travel, rapid media and social media access via the internet, and online availability of court decisions—courts around the world increasingly pay more attention to judicial decisions made in other nations.

In regard to consideration of religious freedom in particular, at Canada's founding its constitution, the *British North America Act* (*BNA Act*),[117] made no provision in regard to religion except the protection of minority religious education rights in each of the four founding

---

116 Several court decisions will be mentioned or footnoted in this chapter, identifying the applicable constitutional/legal principle relevant to religious freedom. In the bibliography, there is a section for Judicial Sources, which includes a brief summary of the key points in regard to each case.

117 *British North America Act, 1867*, 30 & 31 Victoria, c. 3 (U.K.), now *Constitution Act, 1867*, R.S.C. 1985, Appendix II, No. 5.

provinces. Religion was the jurisdiction of the churches and the courts, with Canadian courts following the British tradition on matters of human rights, including in regard to religion. The *BNA Act* assigned jurisdiction for "property and civil rights" to the provinces. The first provincial bill of rights became law in Saskatchewan in 1947. What we today call human rights still have legislative guidelines that vary somewhat from province to province.

At the same time Saskatchewan was working on its Bill of Rights, the United Nations established the Commission on Human Rights, which was tasked with drafting what on December 10, 1948 was passed as Resolution 217, the *Universal Declaration of Human Rights* (the *Declaration*).[118][119] The *Declaration* is not a binding treaty. However, it is regarded as a constitutional document of the United Nations, considered by courts and governments worldwide as part of customary international law[120] that influences the laws, and understanding of the laws, in sovereign nations.

The last paragraph in the preamble of the *Declaration* states:

> The General Assembly proclaims this Universal Declaration of Human Rights as a common standard of achievement for all peoples and all nations, to the end that every individual and every organ of society, keeping this Declaration constantly in mind, shall strive by teaching and education to promote respect for these rights and freedoms and by progressive measures, national and international, to secure their universal and

---

118 The United Nations, *Universal Declaration of Human Rights*, 10 December 1948, GA Res.217 A (III), UN GAOR, 3rd sess., Supp. No. 13, UN Doc. A/810 (1948) 71.

119 This story is told in more detail in Chapter Seven of *Under Siege*, "A Few Words About The Charter."

120 The International Law Commission of the United Nations notes that international law does not require a treaty base and identifies the following sources as examples of evidence for customary international law: international conventions (customary international law underlies treaties and agreements recognizing rules between states that form part of international conventional law), decisions of national and international courts, national legislation, opinions of national legal advisors, diplomatic correspondence, and the practice of international organizations. See: *Report of the International Law Commission to the General Assembly*, Part II. Ways and Means of Making the Evidence of Customary International Law More Readily Available, [1950] 2 Y.B. Int'l L. Comm'n 367, U.N. Doc. A/CN.4/Ser.A/1950/Add.1 (1957), 367–374.

effective recognition and observance, both among the peoples of Member States themselves and among the peoples of territories under their jurisdiction.

Article 18 of the *Declaration* addresses freedom of religion with these words:

Everyone has the right to freedom of thought, conscience and religion; this right includes freedom to change his religion or belief, and freedom, either alone or in community with others and in public or private, to manifest his religion or belief in teaching, practice, worship and observance.

Additionally, in 1976 the United Nations' *International Covenant on Civil and Political Rights*[121] came into force. The *Covenant* also contains an Article 18, with four subsections, which addresses freedom of religion:

1. Everyone shall have the right to freedom of thought, conscience and religion. This right shall include freedom to have or to adopt a religion or belief of his choice, and freedom, either individually or in community with others and in public or private, to manifest his religion or belief in worship, observance, practice and teaching.
2. No one shall be subject to coercion which would impair his freedom to have or to adopt a religion or belief of his choice.
3. Freedom to manifest one's religion or beliefs may be subject only to such limitations as are prescribed by law and are necessary to protect public safety, order, health, or morals or the fundamental rights and freedoms of others.
4. The States Parties to the present Covenant undertake to have respect for the liberty of parents and, when applicable, legal guardians to ensure the religious and moral education of their children in conformity with their own convictions.

---

[121] The United Nations, *International Covenant on Civil and Political Rights*, 19 December 1966, 999 UNTS 171, Can TS 1976 No. 47 (entered into force 23 March 1976).

PART II: IN SOCIETY

In 1982, the *Canadian Charter of Rights and Freedoms* (the *Charter*)[122] was included in the constitutional amendment that brought Canada's constitution from the Parliament at Westminster into the care of the federal and provincial governments, representing the people, of the Dominion of Canada. Included in the *Charter* is Section 2, which states fundamental freedoms, including freedom of religion:

> 2. Everyone has the following fundamental freedoms:
> (*a*) freedom of conscience and religion;
> (*b*) freedom of thought, belief, opinion and expression, including freedom of the press and other media of communication;
> (*c*) freedom of peaceful assembly; and
> (*d*) freedom of association.

No *Charter* freedoms are regarded as absolute, but they are considered by the Supreme Court of Canada to be "broad and jealously guarded."[123] Any limitation of Canadians' freedoms, or other rights noted in the *Charter*, is to be in accordance with Section 1 of the *Charter*.

> 1. The *Canadian Charter of Rights and Freedoms* guarantees the rights and freedoms set out in it subject only to such reasonable limits prescribed by law as can be demonstrably justified in a free and democratic society.

Infringement of *Charter* rights may only occur by actions of the government, i.e. as prescribed by law, because the *Charter* applies to protect Canadians from the actions of the government. For an infringement to be permitted, it must be justified before the courts as being both necessary and minimally impairing the right or freedom at issue.[124] Rights

---

[122] Part I of the *Constitution Act, 1982*.
[123] *Reference re Same-Sex Marriage*, 2004 SCC 79.
[124] *R. v. Oakes*, [1986] 1 SCR 103, sets out a four-part test for assessment of government action that impairs *Charter* right(s).

between citizens continue to be the jurisdiction of the provinces and provincial human rights legislation.[125]

On April 24, 1985, the Supreme Court of Canada issued its first decision commenting on the *Charter* guarantee to freedom of religion. In *R. v. Big M Drug Mart*,[126] the court gave a broad definition of freedom of religion, one that aligns with Article 18 of the UN *Declaration* and Article 18 of the *International Covenant on Civil and Political Rights*.

> 94. A truly free society is one which can accommodate a wide variety of beliefs, diversity of tastes and pursuits, customs and codes of conduct. A free society is one which aims at equality with respect to the enjoyment of fundamental freedoms and I say this without any reliance upon s. 15 of the *Charter*. Freedom must surely be founded in respect for the inherent dignity and the inviolable rights of the human person. *The essence of the concept of freedom of religion is the right to entertain such religious beliefs as a person chooses, the right to declare religious beliefs openly and without fear of hindrance or reprisal, and the right to manifest religious belief by worship and practice or by teaching and dissemination.* But the concept means more than that.
>
> 95. Freedom can primarily be characterized by the absence of coercion or constraint. If a person is compelled by the state or the will of another to a course of action or inaction which he would not otherwise have chosen, he is not acting of his own volition and he cannot be said to be truly free. One of the major purposes of the *Charter* is to protect, within reason, from compulsion or restraint. Coercion includes not only such blatant forms of compulsion as direct commands to act or refrain from acting on pain of sanction, coercion includes indirect forms of control which determine or limit alternative courses of conduct available to others. Freedom in a broad

---

125 Except areas of federal jurisdiction. Federally, the government is also constrained by the *Canadian Bill of Rights* and private actors in fields of federal jurisdiction are accountable under the *Canada Human Rights Act*. The territories are federal jurisdiction, but function much like the provinces and have territorial human rights legislation.
126 *R. v. Big M Drug Mart*, [1985] 1 SCR 295.

sense embraces both the absence of coercion and constraint, and the right to manifest beliefs and practices. Freedom means that, subject to such limitations as are necessary to protect public safety, order, health, or morals or the fundamental rights and freedoms of others, no one is to be forced to act in a way contrary to his beliefs or his conscience.

96. What may appear good and true to a majoritarian religious group, or to the state acting at their behest, may not, for religious reasons, be imposed upon citizens who take a contrary view. The *Charter* safeguards religious minorities from the threat of "the tyranny of the majority."[127]

This broad and robust definition of freedom of religion, which includes worship and is more wide-ranging and public-oriented than worship, is balanced with a finding in paragraph 123 of the decision.

123. ...The values that underlie our political and philosophic traditions demand that every individual be free to hold and to manifest whatever beliefs and opinions his or her conscience dictates, provided *inter alia* only that such manifestations do not injure his or her neighbours or their parallel rights to hold and manifest beliefs and opinions of their own.

The alignment of Canadian law with the *Declaration, Covenant,* and customary international law,[128] including recognition of reasonable limitation of rights,[129] continues to inform the decisions of Canadian courts on freedom of religion. This also marks decisions of the Supreme Court of Canada as relevant to the global understanding of religious freedom.

---

127 Ibid., paragraphs 94–96. Emphasis added.
128 Including, in regard to religious freedom particularly: The United Nations, *International Covenant on Civil and Political Rights*; and *United Nations Declaration on the Elimination of All Forms of Intolerance and of Discrimination based on Religion or Belief*, GA Res.36/55, UN GAOR Supp. (no. 51) 71, UN Doc. A/36/51 (1981).
129 International Commission of Jurists, *A Primer on International Human Rights Law and Standards on the Right to Freedom of Thought, Conscience, Religion or Belief* (International Commission of Jurists, January 2019), 12.

THE STATE, CITIZENS' RIGHTS AND RELIGION

Here, in summary form,[130] are some key principles established by Canada's Supreme Court that are significant for the Canadian understanding of religious freedom, and influential for the understanding of religious freedom in other nations around the world:

- Religious freedom is guaranteed for individuals who have sincerely held religious beliefs, and the personal practices connected with those beliefs are deemed an expression of that freedom.[131]
- Religious freedom has a collective quality, as religion is generally practiced in groups (congregations, denominations, etc.) and through institutions based on a shared religious commitment of both belief and practice.[132]
- Religious groups, organizations, and institutions may establish and enforce their own membership standards, including the right of religious organizations to hire co-religionists (e.g. Roman Catholic teachers at a Roman Catholic school).[133]
- Parents have the authority to raise their children and educate them with the parents' religious beliefs and practices.[134]

---

130 Each of these points gets detailed consideration in Chapters Seven to Sixteen of *Under Siege*.
131 *Syndicat Northcrest v. Amselem*, 2004 SCC 47; *Multani v. Commission scolaire Marguerite-Bourgeoys*, 2006 SCC 6.
132 *R. v. Edwards Books* [1986] 2 SCR 713; *Trinity Western University v. British Columbia College of Teachers*, 2001 SCC 31; *Congrégation des témoins de Jéhovah de St-Jérôme-Lafontaine v. Lafontaine (Village)*, 2004 SCC 48; *Reference re Same-Sex Marriage*, 2004 SCC 79; *Loyola High School v. Quebec (Attorney General)*, 2015 SCC 12; *Highwood Congregation of Jehovah's Witnesses (Judicial Committee) v. Wall*, 2018 SCC 26.
133 *Caldwell v. Stuart*, [1984] 2 SCR 603; *Lakeside Colony of Hutterian Brethren v. Hofer*, [1992] 3 SCR 165; *Trinity Western University v. British Columbia College of Teachers*, 2001 SCC 31; *Alberta v. Hutterian Brethren of Wilson Colony*, 2009 SCC 37; *Highwood Congregation of Jehovah's Witnesses (Judicial Committee) v. Wall*, 2018 SCC 26.
134 *The Queen v. Jones*, [1986] 2 SCR 284; *S.L. v. Commission scolaire des Chênes*, 2012 SCC 7. See also: The United Nations, *Universal Declaration of Human Rights*, Article 26 (3); The United Nations, *International Covenant on Civil and Political Rights*, Article 18, section 4; and The United Nations, *United Nations Declaration on the Elimination of All Forms of Intolerance and of Discrimination based on Religion or Belief*, GA Res.36/55, UN GAOR Supp. (no. 51) 71, UN Doc. A/36/51 (1981), Article 5.

- The state interest in the education of children is that they are being prepared to be good citizens.[135]
- There is a recognized standard for confidential communications between a member of the clergy and a parishioner or other confessor, which requires an expressed understanding of confidentiality by both clergy and parishioner/confessor.[136]
- Sacred texts are not, in and of themselves, hate speech. It is how they are used that might be.[137]
- The state (government and governmental bodies, including the courts) is to be neutral in regard to religious beliefs, neither favouring nor hindering a particular belief, including in the administration of state programs generally available to members of society.[138]
- The state is not to be the arbiter (decision-maker) of religious beliefs.[139]

---

135 *The Queen v.* Jones, [1986] 2 SCR 284; *Ross v. New Brunswick School District No. 36*, [1996] 1 SCR 825; *Trinity Western University v. British Columbia College of Teachers*, 2001 SCC 31; *S.L. v. Commission scolaire des Chênes*, 2012 SCC 7; *Loyola High School v. Quebec (Attorney General)*, 2015 SCC 12.

136 *R. v. Gruenke*, [1991] 3 SCR 263, which applies the "Wigmore Test": "(1) The communications must originate in a confidence that they will not be disclosed; (2) This element of confidentiality must be essential to the full and satisfactory maintenance of the relation between the parties; (3) The relation must be one which in the opinion of the community ought to be sedulously fostered; (4) The injury that would inure to the relation by the disclosure of the communications must be greater than the benefit thereby gained for the correct disposal of litigation." i.e. (1) Both confessor and clergy must have an understood expectation of confidentiality; (2) Confidentiality must be understood to be essential in the relationship (perhaps as a part of church policy); (3) The community—undefined but generally considered as "society" although arguably the religious community—must be of the opinion that confidentiality in the relationship is to be encouraged for reasons that benefit the community, not just the confessor; (4) The injury that would result from disclosure must be greater than what the court would gain by having whatever evidence the court considers would be disclosed.

137 *Saskatchewan (Human Rights Commission) v. Whatcott*, 2013 SCC 11.

138 *R. v. Big M Drug Mart*, [1985] 1 SCR 295; *S.L. v. Commission scolaire des Chênes*, 2012 SCC 7; *Loyola High School v. Quebec (Attorney General)*, 2015 SCC 12.

139 *Syndicat Northcrest v. Amselem*, 2004 SCC 47; *Multani v. Commission scolaire Marguerite-Bourgeoys*, 2006 SCC 6.

- The state cannot compel behaviour contrary to religious beliefs and practices.[140]
- In deliberations on public policy, the positions of all citizens, whether religious or non-religious, are equally legitimate and to be considered by the state.[141]

In addition to freedom of religion, there are other rights of citizenship. Rights of citizenship are important. Like Paul, we do well to know our rights. We cannot predict when such knowledge may be needed and valuable to us.

An emerging trend in several nations, including Canada, is a process of balancing rights when people's identified rights are found to be in conflict or competition with one another. In some situations, government and the courts make a sincere effort to accommodate the competing rights of those concerned, minimizing any infringement. In others, they rank rights based on political or societal popularity, and one person's rights defer to those of another, whether or not any harm was being done. Certainly, in Paul's day, even his rights as a Roman citizen were limited by his chosen religion, Christianity.

It is valuable to know the extent of our rights and any limitations on our freedoms, particularly if we are to maximize our opportunities to contribute to the common good and to share the Gospel. Make the effort to know your rights of citizenship, not just what you think they are but how your government and courts interpret and apply those rights, and, like Paul, how you can appeal to your rights if necessary.

In addition to its responsibility to recognize rights of citizenship, the state may provide other benefits that may influence the earthly citizenship expression of our heavenly citizenship objectives. We will explore some of those benefits, and their potential consequences, next.

---

140 *Reference re Same-Sex Marriage*, 2004 SCC 79.
141 *Chamberlain v. Surrey School District No. 36*, 2002 SCC 86.

Three Takeaways

- Citizenship in a nation-state includes certain rights. Know your rights. Don't assume you do.
- Citizenship rights vary from nation to nation. Your rights don't travel with you outside of your nation.
- Freedom of religion or belief is a right recognized under international law, but not equally applied from nation to nation.

CHAPTER NINE

THE STATE, GOVERNMENT BENEFITS

> *You are the salt of the earth, but if salt has lost its taste, how shall its saltiness be restored? It is no longer good for anything except to be thrown out and trampled under people's feet.*
>
> *You are the light of the world. A city set on a hill cannot be hidden. Nor do people light a lamp and put it under a basket, but on a stand, and it gives light to all in the house. In the same way, let your light shine before others, so that they may see your good works and give glory to your Father who is in heaven.*
>
> —Matthew 5:13–16

WHEN A GOVERNMENT MEDIA RELEASE SAYS TO EXPECT AN ANNOUNCEMENT ON Friday afternoon, it's often an indication that the government wants to announce something while elected opposition representatives aren't present to respond, and knowing the media has already prepared its commentaries for the weekend. When the media release says a press conference is scheduled during Christmas break, when parliamentarians are home and won't return for a month, *and* on a Friday afternoon, pay close attention.

In December 2017, the Government of Canada made just such an announcement.

Typically, the December Canada Summer Jobs (CSJ) announcement is routine, designed to start the clock moving on applications for Canada's long-running program to help fund summer employment for high school and college students.

This day, however, the process took an ideological shift. Applicants for CSJ 2018 funding would be required to attest that their organization supported a right to abortion services (called "reproductive rights" in the newly introduced attestation clause). This right does not exist in Canadian law. It's a controversial matter still debated in the Canadian public square. Additionally, applicants would have to attest that they would not discriminate in hiring "on the basis of sex, religion, race, national or ethnic origin, colour, mental or physical disability, sexual orientation, or gender identity or expression."[142]

Seemingly, it didn't matter that there were recent Supreme Court of Canada decisions requiring government to be neutral in its treatment of citizens and organizations when offering a programme generally available to the public. The constitutional protections of freedom of conscience, freedom of thought, freedom of expression, and freedom of religion were ignored by the government in compelling organizations to hold to the government's ideological position in order to receive funding. It did not seem to matter that the right of religious organizations to hire co-religionists has been established in Canadian human rights law.

This was a multifaceted challenge for churches and faith-based organizations. Many had become dependent on the funding for summer day camps, often hosted by and in local places of worship, for fresh air camps outside the city, for children's ministries and ministries to seniors and people with disabilities, and for other community-oriented service. Historically, the Church has held these activities from May to September when children are out of school and seniors and others want to get outside. The CSJ program aligns with this seasonal demand by encouraging employment of high school and college students.

The December 2017 announcement brought faith leaders from a variety of religions together with common purpose to ask the government to change the new requirement. The government didn't budge.

Should the Church be dependent on government funding for the carrying out of its work? No. But that doesn't mean the Church should

---

142 Cliff Fletcher, "Freedom, Government and Appropriate Response: Canada Summer Jobs," *The Free Methodist Church in Canada*. January 2, 2018 (https://www.fmcic.ca/cliffsnotes-january-2-2018).

not participate in such opportunities. I'll explain that answer in the bulk of this chapter.

Should the Church have equal access to government funding under a program such as Canada Summer Jobs? Yes. In Canada, all citizens and organizations are to be treated as equal by government.

A year later, in its announcement for CSJ 2019,[143] the government changed its position, removing the offending attestation clause. The change was likely the result of several factors: the backlash from religious leaders across the country, a nation in which three-quarters of Canadians still claim religious affiliation;[144] the several court cases started against the government by religious organizations and by businesses that objected to the compulsory language which went beyond legal, human rights, and business requirements;[145] and because the community service programs that ground to a halt in the summer of 2018 resulted in people from every walk of life contacting Members of Parliament with complaints.

There was a time in Canada, and it's still common in other nations, that the Church operated the kinds of community service programs funded by CSJ at its own expense—and greater initiatives as well. Summer programs included Vacation Bible Schools, summer camps, etc. Before we had the massive medical institutions prevalent in Canada's cities, smaller hospitals run by Christian missions dotted the landscape. Sunday schools evolved into day schools run by the Church, often in cooperation with the local community, until they were subsumed by the expanding reach of the state. Children's aid societies and societies for the prevention of cruelty to animals were both started by the Church. The list goes on.

As societal expectations shifted from a demand for small, unobtrusive government, where the people had the answers, to acceptance of large, regulatory bureaucracies involved in almost every sphere of life,

---

[143] John Geddes, "Liberals Move to Defuse Canada Summer Jobs Controversy," *Maclean's*. December 6, 2018 (https://www.macleans.ca/politics/ottawa/liberals-move-to-defuse-canada-summer-jobs-controversy).

[144] "Two-Thirds of Population Declare Christian as Their Religion," *Statistics Canada*. February 19, 2016 (https://www150.statcan.gc.ca/n1/pub/91-003-x/2014001/section03/33-eng.htm).

[145] "Canada Summer Jobs Court Cases," appeal letter, *The Evangelical Fellowship of Canada*. March 7, 2019 (https://www.evangelicalfellowship.ca/Get-involved/Support-the-EFC/Appeal-letters/2019/Canada-Summer-Jobs-Court-Cases).

where government is lobbied to provide the answers, social service initiatives pioneered by the Church for the good of the community have been gradually supplemented, funded, or absorbed by the state.

Still, there was much the Church was better at than government, so government offered financial support to the Church to increase the scope of impact. There is a danger in the Church accepting government funding. The government changes, and the government's position on the faith-based nature of the service it funds also changes.

As I said in *Under Siege*,

> I don't know a single Christian social service ministry that doesn't put the people it serves second, Christ being first. Christian ministries and government bureaucrats have entered into agreements in good faith, knowing that the ministries were doing a better job than the government because of the heart behind the work. It was ministry unto Him, not simply unto them. Times changed, representatives on both sides of the negotiating tables changed, and government spokespersons increasingly pushed beyond the focus of serving people in need to challenging things they didn't understand or accept about the Christian ethos of the increasingly government-dependent organizations.[146]

In Canada, The Salvation Army was one of several churches that recognized a need to establish homes for unwed mothers. Most of these homes provided basic medical care for the safety of mother and child, as well as adoption services. Some homes grew to provide more extensive medical services, eventually becoming a network of hospitals for women.

Near the end of the twentieth century, several provincial governments looked at the expertise for women's health available in Salvation Army hospitals and decided they were the best facilities for the provision of abortion services. The hospitals, however, were an extension of a Christian ministry that held to the biblical position on the sanctity of human life from conception until death. As a result, negotiations took

---

146 Hutchinson, *Under Siege*, 122.

place to turn the Church-founded government-funded hospitals over to government management. The name "Salvation Army Grace" was removed from the buildings.

The Salvation Army was not the only Christian ministry facing these challenges, and the challenges haven't gone away even as the Supreme Court clarified the relevant law. If lawyers and judges don't grasp the legal and constitutional concepts of state neutrality and religious organizations being dealt with on equal footing with other organizations, how could it be expected of elected officials—municipal, provincial, and federal—and government bureaucrats, who were constantly moving into their positions and then moving on? As you might expect, the pastors and Christian leaders on the other side of the negotiations weren't much better prepared.[147]

Christian Horizons is another Canadian ministry. Established to serve people with developmental disabilities by providing care in a residential, rather than institutional, setting, Christian Horizons grew into the largest social service provider in its sector. During this growth, the ministry transitioned from being entirely dependent on private funding to almost entirely dependent on government funding. The government saw the benefits and success of Christian Horizons' approach and decided to fund replication of the care model that was feasible only with the faith-based component.

In the 1990s, Christian Horizons faced a challenge from two employees who contravened the Christian lifestyle standards of the ministry by choosing to live in common-law relationships, rather than marriage. A tribunal upheld the right of the Christian organization to require both faith and lifestyle requirements.[148]

In the 2000s, another Christian Horizons' employee chose to live in a common-law relationship, this time a same-sex relationship. Like

---

147 Ibid., 123.
148 *Parks v. Christian Horizons*, Ontario Human Rights Tribunal, 16 CHRR D/40.

the two women in the 1990s, she chose to challenge the position of her employer in regard to the Christian lifestyle requirements.[149]

> The court affirmed the nature of a religious organization under the [Human Rights] *Code*, including the need for statement of faith and lifestyle policies, but deleted the reference to same-sex relationships and added the requirement that each employee job description indicate the *bona fide* (legitimate) rationale for the responsibilities of that particular position to require agreement with the organization's statement of faith and its lifestyle policy.
>
> At that point, Christian Horizons was faced with the dilemma of continuing to fight the issue of religious practice with a branch of the same government from which it received its funding, or accept the general affirmation by the court of its Christian ministry and get on with serving its more than 1,400 residents, in over 180 locations, employing over 2,500 staff.[150]

It is inevitable that government-funded Christian ministry will eventually face the challenge of a shift in governmental expectations.

In several countries, the operations of the Church are funded substantially or entirely by government. Almost from the time when the Roman Emperor Constantine the Great proclaimed the *Edict of Milan* in 313 A.D., declaring religious tolerance of Christianity within the Roman Empire, the state formed an alliance with the Church that resulted in financial support from the state.

With the Reformation,[151] Western European states often took a position on Christianity that aligned with government funding of the

---

149 *Heintz v. Christian Horizons*, Ontario Human Rights Tribunal, 2008 HRTO 22 (CanLII), 65 C.C.E.L. (3d) 218, 2063 C.H.R.R. 12, *Ontario Human Rights Commission v. Christian Horizons*, 2010 ONSC 2105.
150 Hutchinson, *Under Siege*, 124.
151 The Reformation, also called the Protestant Reformation, was a movement in Western European Christianity in the sixteenth century that challenged the religious and political authority of the Roman Catholic Church, resulting in a separation from the Roman Catholic Church and establishment of what are now called Protestant churches.

Church. Germany, Lutheran. England, Anglican. France, Catholic. And so forth. This has changed in much of the West, but not everywhere.

In Eastern Europe, the Russian Orthodox Church receives significant financial support from government,[152] typifying a common practice for the Church in many former Soviet Bloc states. This is influenced partly because of the continuing societal and political significance of the Church in those nations.[153] Similarly, state-recognized churches in some Western European countries are supported by means of the government taxing those who are registered as church members in order for the government to, in turn, fund Church operations.[154]

In China, registered churches receive state funding and unregistered churches do not. The delegation I travelled with in 2015 attended Sunday morning worship in a beautiful Three-Self Patriotic Movement church building. We were brought in through a special entrance and ushered to reserved seating at the front. Naturally inquisitive, before the service started I rose from my seat to journey to the back of the sanctuary to take some photos of the impressive building. I wandered around a bit, noting there were no children present and no Sunday school classrooms. In China, it is illegal to bring children under the age of eighteen into religious services or to provide them with religious education through a means such as Sunday school. Most recently, the Chinese government has been in the Western news because of its agenda to *sinicize* Christianity, meaning that the Church there is to be retuned so that the expression of Christianity in China aligns with the Chinese government's expectations.[155]

---

152 Anna Kuchma, "Where Does the Russian Orthodox Church Get its Money From?" *Russia Beyond*. March 9, 2016 (https://www.rbth.com/business/2016/03/09/where-does-the-russian-orthodox-church-get-its-money-from_574079).

153 Adam Hug, ed., *Traditional Religion and Political Power: Examining the Role of the Church in Georgia, Armenia, Ukraine and Moldova* (London, UK: The Foreign Policy Centre, 2015).

154 Dalia Fahmy, "European Countries that Have Mandatory Church Taxes Are About as Religious as Their Neighbors that Don't," *Pew Research Centre*. May 9, 2019 (https://www.pewresearch.org/fact-tank/2019/05/09/european-countries-that-have-mandatory-church-taxes-are-about-as-religious-as-their-neighbors-that-dont).

155 Kerry Schottelkorb and Joann Pittman, "China Tells Christianity to Be More Chinese," *Christianity Today*. March 20, 2019 (https://www.christianitytoday.com/news/2019/march/sinicization-china-wants-christianity-churches-more-chinese.html).

PART II: IN SOCIETY

In China, as in many Eastern European and other countries, unregistered churches are considered to be operating outside the requirements of the law.

In North America, we have a different government benefit. In both Canada and the United States, it is common that church properties are exempt from taxation. Additionally, Christian congregations and associations *may* register with the federal government for the privilege of providing receipts to donors, and these receipts allow donors to gain credit for donations and apply them against payment of personal income taxes. This has resulted in donors supporting Christian ministry for tax-planning reasons.

> The advancement of religion has historically been presumed to be of public benefit because of the moral, theological, and ethical framework that religion has provided to the Western world, informing and inspiring its underpinnings and traditions. In our historically Christian-influenced culture, the Church was considered to make a vital contribution to the character and participation of citizens and to the community...
>
> The perception of the Church by Canadian society in the twenty-first century is different than it was even at the close of the twentieth. Some regard the Church as a relic while others see the Church as opposed to the progress of an advancing contemporary Canadian culture.[156]

What will happen to the Church if (some say, when) the government decides that the Church no longer provides the public benefit deserving of having government provide the private benefit that keeps private donor funds out of the state's bank account? Will tax-planning donors continue to give?

> There's nothing wrong with reducing taxes or maximizing charitable capacity by getting those receipts in exchange for our cash. But if the receipts become determinative of our

---

[156] Hutchinson, *Under Siege*, 237–238.

generosity, we might have a problem. The ability to provide or receive a charitable donation receipt is a benefit granted by the federal government. However, the giving imperative is biblical.[157]

Paul writes,

The point is this: whoever sows sparingly will also reap sparingly, and whoever sows bountifully will also reap bountifully. Each one must give as he has decided in his heart, not reluctantly or under compulsion, for God loves a cheerful giver. And God is able to make all grace abound to you, so that having all sufficiency in all things at all times, you may abound in every good work.

—2 Corinthians 9:6–8

The first-century Church did not have financial or other support from the Roman government, nor did it have properties to maintain or the benefit of income tax deductible receipts.

The danger the Church encounters by accepting government benefits for the work of the Church is not in the acceptance but in the dependence. If the Church becomes dependent on, and thus subject to, the government for the work of the Church, we risk being influenced by extrabiblical requirements imposed by government, or being faced with government assuming, and perhaps inappropriately altering, the work entirely.

It is a sensible exercise to regularly contemplate how government-dependent are the ministries you lead or back, and what might be done proactively to minimize risks of losing government support.

Let us be mindful that in doing good for others we are not agents of government but stewards, stewards of the savour of Christ in all we are and do (Matthew 5:13–16). We'll reflect more on that stewardship in the following chapters.

---

157 Ibid., 236.

Three Takeaways

- Government funding/support for the Church carries the risk of the government cutting the cashflow.
- Government funding for the Church may result in government seeking to direct the teaching and practices of the Church.
- The Church is not an agent of government.

CHAPTER TEN

THE CHURCH, LIFESTYLE OF GENEROSITY

Bring the full tithe into the storehouse, that there may be food in my house. And thereby put me to the test, says the Lord of hosts, if I will not open the windows of heaven for you and pour down for you a blessing until there is no more need.

—Malachi 3:10

Soon afterward he [Jesus] went on through cities and villages, proclaiming and bringing the good news of the kingdom of God. And the twelve were with him, and also some women who had been healed of evil spirits and infirmities: Mary, called Magdalene, from whom seven demons had gone out, and Joanna, the wife of Chuza, Herod's household manager, and Susanna, and many others, who provided for them [some manuscripts say "him"] out of their means.

—Luke 8:1–3

Each one must give as he has decided in his heart, not reluctantly or under compulsion, for God loves a cheerful giver.

—2 Corinthians 9:7

MY GRANDSON CHANGED MY LIFE. YES, I KNOW THAT'S WHAT ALL grandparents say. But my grandson really did change my life. How I live. The way I plan. My goals. John changed the trajectory of my life without changing the Centre of my life. In fact, my grandson has influenced my world in a way that navigates me closer to Jesus.

An active boy who lives with Grandma and Grandpa, John was born with a non-functioning pituitary gland, the thermostat for the endocrine system. He requires a selection of custom-mixed-and-measured medications every day to stay alive, to keep his brain functioning, and to grow. John is also legally (but not totally) blind, autistic, and has been diagnosed with global developmental delay.

Our world has been reoriented. We are still centred around Jesus, but the next concentric circle in our lives includes a committed focus on John.

In his book *Uniquely Human*, autism specialist Barry Prizant captures a helpful perspective on the concept Christians call *imago Dei*, i.e. all people are made in the image of God (Genesis 1:26–27). Prizant uses words that encourage a paradigm shift for those of us who are *typical* humans:

> Autism isn't an illness. It's a different way of being human. Children with autism aren't sick; they are progressing through developmental stages as we all do. To help them, we don't need to change them or fix them. We need to work to understand them, and then change what *we* do.[158]

None of the things that make John atypical diminish his humanity.

Prizant makes another point that is too often missed by typical humans about humans we live with who are atypical in developmental capacities or behaviours:

> There is no such thing as autistic behavior. These are all *human* behaviors and *human* responses based on a person's experiences.[159]

Prizant's remarks could just as easily have been made about blindness, deafness, Down syndrome, foetal alcohol syndrome, or other so-called "disorders." My behaviours are also based on my experiences. John's benchmarks aren't less than those of other humans; they are

---

158   Barry M. Prizant, with Tom Fields-Meyer, *Uniquely Human: A Different Way of Seeing Autism* (New York, NY: Simon & Schuster Paperbacks, 2015), 4.
159   Ibid., 5.

THE CHURCH, LIFESTYLE OF GENEROSITY

uniquely John's, just as mine are uniquely mine and yours are uniquely yours. My role, as any parent or grandparent with a child, is to help John become the best *John* he can be based on who he is, not based on societal expectations, diagnoses, or limitation labels.

The essence of human rights expressed in international declarations, national constitutions, and countless courtrooms around the globe is founded in the concept of *imago Dei*, the idea that human dignity isn't something to be achieved but something we have inherently because we are image-bearers.

John has changed my life by inspiring a fresh wind of *other*-focused generosity to blow into my life. Generosity is often thought of as financial, but it is more than financial. Generosity is also about transformation of the heart and mind, an adjustment in attitude, commitment of time, and the giving of self and resources in a manner pointedly about assessing how purposeful we are in our consideration of others.

An African proverb says, "It takes a village to raise a child." This has proven true with John, as it has in the lives of myriad other children, typical and atypical. John has inspired and revealed multiple facets of generosity expressed by a number of people in a variety of ways.

In addition to family, John's village includes a church-family. Our church-family know John, love him, and extend generosity to him in several ways.

Barry and Joyce, who live and teach the lifestyle of generosity as a biblical principle, were an encouragement during John's prolonged initial hospital stay, and they are a continuing presence in his life. One couple coached us in how to spot signs of concern. They have two children with the same life-threatening condition John has. A friend my age who has the same condition is a living message of hope for the future, and John enjoys a grilled cheese sandwich and milk from him when we go to visit. It was great to have a nursing student as a babysitter, someone who could administer John's medications for an evening out. When John needed a specialized therapy bike to facilitate the building of muscle intended by one medication, people who love him (and us) met his need. John also attends a Catholic school where our extended church-family (we're Protestant) are attentive to his development.

These kindnesses come from the heart. Along with the many more who pray and care, these church-family members express a lifestyle of generosity that testifies to Jesus-in-residence.

With the birth of their son Steven in 1963, a Baptist evangelist named Jim Reese and his wife Adrienne started thinking about how we care for people with developmental disabilities in Ontario, Canada. They were particularly interested in the idea of a Christian organization that would provide a full range of services in a home setting in the same kind of community in which they themselves lived.

In November 1964, Jim wrote in a letter to Adrienne,

> If God does have such a ministry in mind, now is the time to be getting actively involved in promoting it. In just a few years Steven will be ready for it. And even more, many children from Christian homes are already in need.[160]

Within a year, they would experience a different kind of birth. Christian Horizons, mentioned in the previous chapter, was established to provide just such a Christian care environment. The Reeses and the families who joined with them extended their lifestyle of generosity to create homes for their children throughout life, as well as for the children of others.

Christian Horizons operates more than two hundred residences in Ontario and Saskatchewan, and Christian Horizons Global has impacted more than three hundred thousand lives in sixty communities around the world.[161]

Half a world away, around the same time Jim was writing to Adrienne, another Canadian, a Roman Catholic philosopher, was experiencing the call to a similar ministry, this one of a Christian-influenced secular nature. Jean Vanier recounts his story in *Becoming Human*:

---

160 Ulrich Frisse, *Building Communities of Belonging: The Ongoing Story of Christian Horizons* (Kitchener, ON: Historical Branding Solutions, Inc., 2016), 19. Letter by Jim Reese to Adrienne Reese, November 13, 1964.
161 "How It All Began," *Christian Horizons*. Date of access: May 13, 2019 (https://www.christian-horizons.org/who-we-are/history).

Then in April 1964 I went to visit a holy priest—a man of God. He was chaplain to a small institution for people with intellectual disabilities. It was there I discovered the plight of men and women who had been put aside, looked down upon, sometimes laughed at or scorned. They were seen as misfits of nature, not as human beings.

Touched and hurt by the way so many were treated, I was able to buy a little house in a village north of Paris and to welcome two men with disabilities from a sad and violent institution…

And so the first community of L'Arche was born.[162]

Today, there are 149 L'Arche communities in thirty-seven countries.[163]

Vanier grasped the original philosophical and theological implications of sacred and secular. The sacred, within the vocations of the Church, and secular, work outside the Church, are both to be genuine expressions of our Christlikeness. Following in the footsteps of the carpenter from Nazareth (Jesus, Mark 6:3), the tentmaker from Tarsus (Paul, Acts 18:3) or continuing in our work without the public preaching component (slaves,[164] Colossians 3:22–24; and labourers, 1 Thessalonians 4:11–12), all that we do is testament to Him.

---

162 Jean Vanier, *Becoming Human* (Toronto, ON: House of Anansi Press Inc., 2008), 1–2.
163 "A Brief History of L'Arche," *L'Arche Canada*. Date of access: May 13, 2019 (https://www.larche.ca/about-larche/our-history).
164 In Paul's time, "slave" was a legitimate societal status. Paul, a Roman citizen, even described himself as a *doulos* of Christ Jesus (Romans 1:1). The radical nature of the gospel resulted in Paul communicating the powerful message that in Jesus all are equal, that in heavenly citizenship there is no status of slave or free (Galatians 3:28). He also wrote to Philemon to receive Onesimus, Philemon's slave, as a brother in Christ (Philemon 16). *Doulos* is translated most frequently as "slave," and also as servant or bondservant, i.e. one who is subservient to another (James Strong, *Strong's Exhaustive Concordance, Greek Dictionary of the New Testament*, #1401). The preface to the ESV notes that "a particular difficulty is presented when words in biblical Hebrew and Greek refer to ancient practices and institutions that do not correspond directly to those in the modern world." One of those words is *doulos*. For that reason, in the ESV and other translations the word *doulos* is translated variously as slave, servant, and bondservant, with an effort being made to align with the context of the text, footnoting the range of meanings.

Vanier, the Reeses, and our church-family have all offered contemporary expressions of the lifestyle of generosity. There are many more typical and atypical humans who need a place of acceptance and care. An individual and community lifestyle of generosity is an available characteristic of following Jesus, who gave all and gives all. Jesus inspires generosity.

In *Unimaginable: What Our World Would Be Like Without Christianity*, Jeremiah Johnston recounts a letter written in 1 B.C. from a Roman migrant worker named Hilarion, working in Alexandria, Egypt, to his pregnant wife, Alis, who was about three hundred twenty kilometres (two hundred miles) away at their home in Oxyrhynchus. After conveying his love and noting that he would be delayed in returning home, Hilarion wrote,

> If—may you have good luck—you should give birth; if it is a boy, keep it; if it is a girl, throw it out...[165]

Johnston then continues, providing some societal context:

> *Throw it out?!* Hilarion's shocking command to his wife, to throw out the newborn if a girl, reflected a common practice of infanticide among Greeks and Romans. Girls, as well as boys, did go to work at young ages and help the family get by. Still, unwanted girls and infants with birth defects and deformities were routinely cast out to die of exposure either to the elements or to wild animals. (In the face of great danger, though, we know that early Christians roamed the streets at night to rescue abandoned children before wild dogs or other animals got to them...)[166]

Christians, followers of a religion that was illegal in the first-century Roman Empire, met to worship in private, to grow their relationship with Jesus and with other Christians, and they expressed *love your neighbour* in meaningful, and countercultural, ways, demonstrating

---

[165] Johnston, *Unimaginable*, 26.
[166] Ibid.

compassion for the society in which they lived. *Imago Dei*, seeing the image of God in all people, inspired a risky generosity, including accepting a lifetime responsibility for abandoned children and, as noted earlier, caring for brothers and sisters, widows, and orphans in the church-family who were in need.

Understanding humans and human needs in the unchanging context of *imago Dei* inspires generosity in loving God, loving one another, and loving our neighbours as ourselves. Sometimes generosity is extravagant, such as demonstrated in the true story about Mary anointing Jesus in Bethany, one of the few events in Jesus' life that is recorded in all four gospels (Matthew 26:6–13; Mark 14:3–9; Luke 7:36–50; John 12:1–8). Yes, I know some scholars speculate that there were two women, one anointing his head on one occasion and another his feet. If they're right, that only doubles the extravagant generosity inspired by Jesus!

In his book *Gospel Patrons*, American author and speaker John Rinehart poses two questions that can inform and challenge our own generosity.

> First, *How has God worked through people to change the world?* And second, *How do we become those kind of people?*[167]

Rinehart describes gospel patrons as more than philanthropists, because their focus is not simply on supporting good causes, but supporting causes with eternal focus.[168] He describes the generosity of Mary, Joanna, and Susanna as told in Luke 8:1–3 and notes,

> These three women who were "with Him" also "provided for them out of their means." They were involved and invested in Jesus' ministry.[169]

This is more than financial giving; it is generosity of time and personal commitment, as well as money. The lifestyle of generosity shown

---

[167] John Rinehart, *Gospel Patrons: People Whose Generosity Changed the World* (Minneapolis, MN: Reclaimed Publishing, 2016), 20.
[168] Ibid., 24.
[169] Ibid., 29.

by Mary, Joanna, and Susanna facilitated the ministry of Jesus of Nazareth. It wasn't just a good cause, but an eternal one!

About Priscilla and Aquila, Rinehart writes,

> In the book of Acts we meet Priscilla and Aquila, a married couple in the early church, who were business people. But that did not stop them from engaging in God's business to advance the gospel. They hosted a church in their house, came alongside a well-known preacher named Apollos and helped him with his theology, and partnered with the Apostle Paul at the risk of their own lives. (See these stories in Acts 18:1–3, 26 and 1 Cor. 16:19).[170]

Tentmakers like Paul, Priscilla, and Aquila had a lifestyle of generosity that made a difference in the life of the first-century Church—and the twenty-first century Church.

If the Reeses and Jean Vanier seem like bigger difference-makers than you think you can be, remember that more than half a century has passed since their small beginnings.

Here's one more story, from the twenty-first century.

My friend Ritchie does odd jobs and enjoys life. He had little, he had much, and he lost it all. In the process, Ritchie had a divine encounter with Jesus that changed his life. He remembers what it was like to live on the streets, so he volunteers to spend time with people who are street-engaged today. Some see derelicts. Ritchie sees humans, *imago Dei*.

From time to time, Ritchie takes pizza downtown to his street friends, inviting donations from others to help cover costs. For Mother's Day, he collects purses that people are willing to part with and fills them with the items most women consider part of their daily fare. He distributes the treasure-filled purses to women who won't likely get a card or a call from family, but they will get a purse, and maybe a hug, in Jesus' name. Ritchie's generosity invites the generosity of the people who provide pizza, purses, merchandise, cash, coffee cards, a ride downtown to make it happen, and those who join him in the giveaway.

---

170 Ibid.

In his book *The Power of Generosity*, Dave Toycen, the former CEO of World Vision Canada, writes, "being generous is about more than money; it involves our time, influence and expertise as well."[171] My friend Ritchie might not be CEO of an international Christian ministry, but the principle is the same, just as it was for the Reeses, Jean Vanier, Mary, Joanna, Susanna, Priscilla, and Aquila—and the people who are generous to our John. There remains a biblical responsibility for Christians to consider and express stewardship of time, influence, expertise, and money by living a life of generosity and supporting just causes, with eternal goals in mind.

Toycen writes,

> Generosity is not lost; compassion is not discarded, because most of us realize that if you go back far enough, all of us benefited from someone who helped us in a way that was not required. Generosity pays dividends.[172]

First-century Christians had neither the support of the Roman government nor the benefit of income tax deduction receipts. But there were needs, Old Testament Scripture that informed their understanding of giving, and the teaching of Paul and others. The Church was challenged to advance the concept of giving beyond the Old Testament tithe that kept the temple running (Malachi 3:10) to adopt a standard of lifestyle generosity that changes the world (e.g. 2 Corinthians 9:6–15), sometimes transforming the world of just one person, and other times having an impact in the world of many.

Living and giving cheerfully of ourselves and our resources makes a difference. As Paul wrote about the lifestyle of generosity he encountered in Corinth, where he first met Priscilla and Aquila, *"Now thanks be to God for His indescribable gift [which is precious beyond words]!"* (2 Corinthians 9:15, AMP).

---

[171] Dave Toycen, *The Power of Generosity: How to Transform Yourself and Your World* (Toronto, ON: HarperCollins Publishers Ltd., 2004), 120.
[172] Ibid., 124

An eternity-focused lifestyle of earthly generosity is powerfully influential. Indescribably so. In fact, it is too strong to be conveyed in mere words. But words can convey something of it. So let me give the final words of this chapter to Saint (Mother) Teresa of Calcutta:

> Let us not be satisfied with just giving money. Money is not enough, money can be got, but they need your hearts to love them. So, spread your love everywhere you go.[173]

Three Takeaways

- The essence of human rights, and in fact all humanity, is *imago Dei*.
- When a Christian agrees that people experiencing adversity are made in the image of God, we are compelled by compassion to do something.
- Christians will find ways to give of ourselves and our resources, directly or in relationship with trusted others, to assist those whose needs draw our kindness.

---

[173] Mother Teresa of Calcutta, *A Gift for God* (London, UK: Collins, 1975), 54.

CHAPTER ELEVEN

THE CHURCH, PUBLIC ENGAGEMENT

A false balance is an abomination to the Lord, but a just weight is his delight.

—Proverbs 11:1

There was a man in the land of Uz whose name was Job, and that man was blameless and upright, one who feared God and turned away from evil.

—Job 1:1

So whatever you wish that others would do to you, do also to them, for this is the Law and the Prophets.

—Matthew 7:12

IN THE LATTER YEARS OF THE TWENTIETH CENTURY, A FRESH WIND OF THE Spirit[174] was blowing a few blocks from the Lester B. Pearson International Airport in Toronto. A word of warning spread quickly. I resolved to stay away from the *strange fire*, as some called it, burning in our city. Like Moses drawn to a burning bush in an unlikely location, people travelled to Pearson by the thousands and tens of thousands to visit the Toronto Airport Vineyard—subsequently called Toronto Airport Christian

---

[174] See John 3:8: "The wind [the same Greek word means both wind and spirit] blows where it wishes, and you hear its sound, but you do not know where it comes from or where it goes." See: James Strong, *Strong's Exhaustive Concordance, Greek Dictionary of the New Testament,* #4151 (*pneuma,* a current of air, i.e. breath [blast] or a breeze; by analogy or figuratively, a spirit).

Fellowship, and now Catch The Fire, Toronto Airport—to experience "the Toronto blessing."[175]

Around that time, I allowed my work to overload my life. I burned out. The fire was burning near the airport as my personal flames flickered only half an hour away. While on a six-month leave of absence from The Salvation Army's legal department, I was convinced to risk a visit to *that church*. The first night, a years-earlier three-week residential school on the theology of *the* Holy Spirit was met by an intimate personal experience with Holy Spirit.[176] God had prepared me with the truth of the theology to accept the authenticity of the personal experience. Still, the experience shifted my theology.

Shortly after my return to the office, I sought advice from a friend who had a more expansive theological education. Sitting across from Bill, at his desk, he noted, "Don, The Salvation Army's theology is long and wide, like an airport runway." An apt analogy, I thought. "But it's still possible to go off the edge. And you, my friend, have gone off the edge."

A few months later, I was given an award for fifteen years of commendable service. Within weeks, I was given my walking papers. Off the edge.

I might have landed off The Salvation Army's runway at that time (although it has since been expanded to be more theologically accommodating), but I was still, figuratively speaking, at the Christian airport. I had no idea at the time that this was a necessary step in my spiritual growth. I need to gain humility and a new network connecting me to the global Church, beyond my one denominational experience. I needed to search the Scriptures to develop my understanding of what it meant to trust God and be who He had called me to be, without a guaranteed-to-the-penny income to fall back on. And I needed to take a new route to public service and public policy engagement I would not have considered before.

---

175 Guy Chevrau, *Catch the Fire: The Toronto Blessing, an experience of renewal and revival* (Toronto, ON: HarperPerennial, 1995).
176 Relationally, I knew God the Father lovingly as "Father," and God the Son by His name, Jesus. Now God the Holy Spirit was affectionately known to me as "Holy Spirit."

Within a year, Gloria and I found ourselves moving toward leading a church plant in Markham, just north of Toronto. The congregation made a commitment to cover our housing costs, but I would be bi-vocational, a pastor working at another job to meet life expenses.

Eric, a Christian friend who owns a funeral home, offered me a position doing fill-in-the-gap work while I sorted out the next steps. I drove hearse and processional cars (I had the required license), washed vehicles, took flowers to the cemetery, and greeted families at funerals. Eric is a good character guy, a businessman with a reputation above reproach. As part of his team, it was clear he expected the same from me.

Around the same time, a mutual friend, Don Cousens, then-mayor of Markham, was spearheading an initiative called Character Community. The Character Community Foundation had been established in 2001 and Don, a former Presbyterian minister, perceived its concept to be about encouraging people to learn and apply biblical character principles in school, business, and neighbourhood in order to build caring communities in York Region, which was expanding rapidly at the time. Pastors and Christian leaders were quick to be supportive. The principles may have been drawn from Scripture, but they are broadly accepted in other religious communities as well, so many readily joined in. The school board saw it as an opportunity to extend instruction on principles of good citizenship.

Here are the twelve character attributes, one for each month:

- Optimism: I will maintain a positive attitude, look on the brighter side of situations and seek opportunities in the face of adversity.
- Initiative: I will recognize what needs to be done and do it, without prompting from others.
- Perseverance: I will not give up when things get tough. I will stick to my goals and work hard to achieve them, despite obstacles and challenges.
- Respect: I will treat myself and others with consideration, high regard and dignity.

- Responsibility: I will be accountable for my actions, be reliable and keep my commitments.
- Honesty: I will be sincere, trustworthy and truthful.
- Integrity: I will do what is right and ensure there is no difference between what I say and what I do.
- Compassion: I will do whatever is necessary to heal the hurts of others. I will strive to understand and be sensitive to their feelings.
- Courage: I will stand up for my beliefs and principles and face challenges, fear and difficulty with fortitude.
- Inclusiveness: I will work to build a community where everyone feels included, empowered and valued for his or her unique contributions.
- Fairness: I will treat others in a just, equitable and unbiased manner.
- Humility: I am outwardly focused, with a true interest in others. I am mindful and my values guide my actions.[177]

When we, as Christians, engage in business, education, media, government, sports, and/or the arts, including entertainment, aren't these what people expect of us as followers of Jesus?

In the preface to his 1965 critique of the major traditional denominations in the Canadian Protestant Church—at one time the evangelical denominations that were key to nation-building during Canada's first century—journalist and author Pierre Berton wrote,

> I hope it will be understood that, though this book is a critical one, the criticism of the Church springs out of a general context which is my own belief that Christianity has shaped Western man for the better, and that without Christianity we would be a poorer and less-inspired people.[178]

---

[177] *Character Community, York Region*. Date of access: May 17, 2019 (https://www.charactercommunity.com).

[178] Pierre Berton, *The Comfortable Pew: A Critical Look at the Church in the New Age* (Toronto, ON: McLelland and Stewart, 1965), 13.

Berton's findings for the individual might be summarized in the disappointing observation (and confrontational statement): "Large numbers of nominal Christians are no longer either very hot or very cold, for the virus that has weakened the Church is apathy."[179] This apathy, or disinterest in the things of God and Church among *nominal Christians*, was reflected in a stepping away from the kinds of principles and character qualities that, four decades later, Don Cousens would seek to instill through the Character Community initiative.

In his book *Real Christianity*, William Wilberforce, the British Member of Parliament famous for his battle against the slave trade, referred to this nominal Christianity as *cultural Christianity*, noting, "You might know some of the basic facts about Christianity but have no idea how those facts should apply to your life."[180] He went further, stating, "*Their Christianity is not Christianity.*"[181]

Miroslav Volf, director of the Yale University Center for Faith and Culture, in his book *A Public Faith*, calls this nominal or cultural Christianity by the term "thin Christianity,"[182] which I think of as kind of a veneer of Christianity, somewhat like a bookcase or desk that appears to be made of wood but is not solid to the depth of its core.

Bearing in mind this notion of nominal Christianity, Berton follows comments on the Church's failed role in regard to political leadership with a chapter on business leadership in which he presents what is a continuing challenge for the Church, whether Protestant, Catholic, or Orthodox—namely, compartmentalization:

> Is it possible that this failure to accept responsibility in political matters stems from a long-standing mental compartmentalization that sees no connection between what is said in church on

---

179 Ibid., 29.
180 William Wilberforce, *Real Christianity: A Paraphrase in Modern English of a Practical View of the Prevailing Religious System of Professed Christians in the Higher and Middle Classes in This Country, Contrasted with Real Christianity* (Ventura, CA; Regal Books, 2006), 19. Originally published in 1797, revised and updated by Bob Beltz.
181 Ibid., 165.
182 Miroslav Volf, *A Public Faith: How Followers of Christ Should Serve the Common Good* (Grand Rapids, MI: Brazos Press, 2011), 39–41.

> Sunday and what is done at the office on Monday? For centuries the idea has prevailed that religion is a personal matter, concerned with the private and not the public side of life...
>
> The Protestant emphasis on purely personal salvation has brought about a separation of the business community from the religious community and allowed the Christian businessman to think on two levels. The Christian virtues to which he pays lip service on Sunday go unrecognized in the harsh cut-and-thrust of his weekday life.[183]

What Berton described is the failure of the Church to address, and perhaps instead contribute to, the idea of a private/public separation, a compartmentalization of our private and public selves.

> The businessman and the politician are measured by the Church not in terms of how they conduct their lives or their businesses but in terms of how often they attend the religious club, how active they are in the parish, and how much money they donate to various religious causes.[184]

In response to his diagnosis, Berton's proposed solution was that "for this New Age we need a new kind of Church. The mentality of the New Age is secular, not religious."[185] The Church would need to jettison what he considered the institutional trappings and myths of an ancient era, and focus on "Christian love, in all its flexibility, with all of its concern for real people rather than for any fixed set of rigid principles,"[186] or face "a persecution that would rid the Church of those of little faith."[187]

Persecution may be the result of faithfulness, but it's preferable to a Church, if we can call it that, which would remove Father, Son, and Holy Spirit from the life of the Christian, who would accordingly, in the words of Wilberforce, no longer be a Christian. Wilberforce, instead of

---

183 Berton, *Comfortable Pew*, 50.
184 Ibid., 51.
185 Ibid., 139.
186 Ibid., 141.
187 Ibid., 143.

stepping away from historic Christianity, reflected on the need to develop an authentic faith, real Christianity, with an understanding of sound doctrine and life application.

Similarly, Volf suggests the answer to the problem of a *thin* faith is a *thick* faith, noting that

> the more the Christian faith matters to its adherents as faith that maps a way of life, and the more they practice it as an ongoing tradition with strong ties to its origins and history, and with clear cognitive and moral content, the better off we will be.[188]

This kind of faith is solid to the core and informs every part of life, as opposed to being a veneer of Christianity, adapted to culture.

While I disagree with Berton's suggested solution to address the failings of what he calls "the comfortable pew," and I think I'm in good company doing so, his 1965 observations of pitfalls for which the Church should be mindful and deal with remain relevant.

> Though Christ clearly intended the opposite, churchgoing appears to put more emphasis on formalized religious observance than it does on ethical relationships…
>
> It has all but been forgotten that Christianity began as a revolutionary religion whose followers embraced an entirely different set of values from those held by other members of society. Those original values are still in conflict with the values of the contemporary society…[189]

The challenge is to live with consistency between our privately held faith and our publicly lived life—living a public faith, as it were. Such consistency and integrity is vital to the witness of the Church in our real life daily engagement with our neighbours away from the comfortable pew of Sunday morning worship and the comfortable chair of private daily devotions.

---

188 Volf, *Public Faith*, 40.
189 Berton, *Comfortable Pew*, 85, 94.

PART II: IN SOCIETY

As members of society, if our witness for Jesus Christ is to be consistent from Monday to Saturday, in addition to our Sunday celebration, our personally held Christian beliefs must translate into private and public ethical practices in business, education, media, government, sports, the arts, entertainment, etc. Our interactions with family, friends, and neighbours, both local and global, need to be infused with the character of Jesus that has been birthed and is developing within us as we grow in our relationship with Him and with His Church.

In *Mere Christianity*,[190] Irish scholar and lay theologian C.S. Lewis suggests we be mindful of the four cardinal virtues in our public engagement: prudence, temperance, justice, and fortitude:[191]

> Prudence means practical common sense, taking the trouble to think out what you are doing and what is likely to come of it…
>
> Temperance referred not specially to drink, but to all pleasures; and it meant not abstaining, but going the right length and no further…
>
> Justice… is the old name for everything we should now call "fairness"; it includes honesty, give and take, truthfulness, keeping promises, and all that side of life…
>
> And Fortitude includes both kinds of courage—the kind that faces danger as well as the kind that "sticks it" under pain. "Guts" is perhaps the nearest modern English. You will notice, of course, that you cannot practise any of the other virtues very long without bringing this one into play.[192]

Application of these virtues by the Christian means that he or she need not wait for the lead of the clergy or other church authorities on matters of business and social morality. Lewis was convinced that when people suggested the Church ought to give direction, "they ought to mean that some Christians—those who happen to have the

---

[190] C.S. Lewis, *Mere Christianity* (London, UK: Fontana Books, 1952).
[191] Traditionally, the seven virtues of the Church are the four cardinal virtues (prudence, temperance, justice, fortitude) and the three theological virtues (faith, hope, charity).
[192] Lewis, *Mere Christianity*, 70–72.

right talents—should be economists and statesmen" and that the "application of Christian principles, say, to trade unionism or education, must come from Christian trade unionists and Christian schoolmasters: just as Christian literature comes from Christian novelists and dramatists..."[193]

In short, Christians are best equipped for public engagement by a sincere, deep, developing, and intelligent commitment to follow Jesus in all of life. The Church is where that equipping is fostered.

In late April 2013, a friend invited me to join him at a May 3 luncheon at the Toronto Board of Trade. Another friend had committed to go and the idea was that we would make it a one-day Ottawa-Toronto-Ottawa road trip. I sometimes cringe when I think about the gap that might have been torn in the Canadian religious freedom team if Albertos, André, and I had experienced misadventure instead of adventure on that day.

The Toronto event was a conversation about the continuing threats to global capitalism following the 2008 global financial crisis. The participants were Father Raymond J. de Souza, editor-in-chief of *Convivium Magazine*; Mark Carney, completing his 2008 to 2013 term as Governor of the Bank of Canada; and Roger Martin, dean of the Rotman School of Management at the University of Toronto. All three traced the world financial crisis that began in 2008 to a failure of individual personal ethics.

In his talk, Carney noted five Cs[194] necessary for recovery and stability, including,

> The fifth "C"—core values—is the responsibility of the financial sector and its leaders. Their behaviour during the crisis demonstrated that many were not being guided by sound core values...
>
> More fundamentally, to think that compensation arrangements can ensure virtue is to miss the point entirely. Integrity cannot be legislated, and it certainly cannot be bought. It must come from within...

---

193 Ibid., 75.
194 Mark Carney's five Cs: capital, clarity, capitalism, connecting with clients, and core values.

To help rebuild that foundation, bankers, like all of us, need to avoid compartmentalization or what the former chair of HSBC, Stephen Green, calls "the besetting sin of human beings." When we compartmentalize, we divide our life into different realms, each with its own set of rules. Home is distinct from work; ethics from law.[195]

Sound familiar?

In his comments, de Souza offered these thoughts on what Carney had said:

Integrity cannot be legislated and it certainly cannot be bought. It must come from within. But from within what? If regulation is insufficient, we must rely on the men and women of finance to regulate themselves. It's the Governor's argument about individual responsibility. They must do it from within.

But one might ask, then, what about those core values? If they must do it from within by their necessary core values, what is, in fact, at the core? The great theologian of the free society and free economy, Michael Novak, who is now in retirement—I recommend his works—taught us that the free market does what it does extremely well. It creates wealth, allocates resources etc., but it does not do metaphysics. That is to say, it does not provide from within itself a logic for the virtues that it actually requires to operate efficiently.

Those have to come from without, from outside of the market, from the realm of ethics, or for many people, faith. As Novak used to put it, the altar of the free market is empty. That is, the market is not supposed to provide us with a god or even with a meaning for life, but if there is no god somewhere

---

[195] Raymond J. de Souza and Mark Carney, Roger Martin, "God, Greed & Gaming." *Convivium Magazine*, June 7, 2013 (https://www.convivium.ca/articles/god-greed-gaming).

else that provides those things then the market can easily be turned into a god itself, to catastrophic effect.[196]

Let's step back to the first-century A.D. I think one of the reasons Priscilla and Aquila could continue their business as tentmakers after being identified as members of a controversial religious sect was because their customers knew their business practices to be exemplary. Being people with unimpeachable good character allowed others to trust them personally and in their business operations. That trust also made them ideal as educators for Apollos the evangelist (Acts 18:24–26). Similarly, in Thyatira, Lydia's reputation as a respected businesswoman was so good that she was known citywide simply by her first name (Acts 16:14).

Paul summarized this citizenship lesson succinctly:

Whatever you do, work heartily, as for the Lord and not for men, knowing that from the Lord you will receive the inheritance as your reward.
—Colossians 3:23–24

As Christians, our public life, including in whatever line of work we engage, is to align with our personal faith, *as for the Lord*. That's character, of the good variety. The influence of our character is experienced in every public interaction, and beyond.

Three Takeaways

- Christian character counts in every area of life: home, school, work, and play.
- *Thicken* your Christianity and you will strengthen your character.
- Exercising common sense, moderation, fairness, and fortitude will cultivate a good reputation in all areas of life.

---

[196] Ibid.

CHAPTER TWELVE

THE CHURCH, POLITICS

Therefore render to Caesar the things that are Caesar's, and to God the things that are God's.

—Matthew 22:21

First of all, then, I urge that supplications, prayers, intercessions, and thanksgivings be made for all people, for kings and all who are in high positions, that we may lead a peaceful and quiet life, godly and dignified in every way. This is good, and it is pleasing in the sight of God our Savior...

—1 Timothy 2:1–3

Be subject for the Lord's sake to every human institution, whether it be to the emperor as supreme, or to governors as sent by him to punish those who do evil and to praise those who do good. For this is the will of God, that by doing good you should put to silence the ignorance of foolish people. Live as people who are free, not using your freedom as a cover-up for evil, but living as servants of God. Honor everyone. Love the brotherhood. Fear God. Honor the emperor.

—1 Peter 2:13–17

POLITICS, WHETHER IN CHURCH LEADERSHIP OR NATIONAL GOVERNANCE, IS supposed to be about people. Serving the people. Looking out for the best interests of all constituents. But too often it's more about power than governance. Part of our sinful nature is the desire to be the greatest

PART II: IN SOCIETY

by having dominance over others rather than by serving them (Matthew 20:25–28; Luke 22:24–27).

In *Under Siege*, I shared the following story about one encounter with the *power* of politics.

> Shortly after joining The Evangelical Fellowship of Canada's public policy team in October 2006, I made a visit to Ottawa. My first day was rushed, but that evening I decided to take a walk up to Parliament Hill in the brisk October air. As I walked north on Metcalfe Street, the Peace Tower grew into the Centre Block and then the West and East Blocks, with the Langevin Block on my right. I touched a cornerstone of the Langevin Block, the office building which houses the Prime Minister's office, before heading across the street. I could sense the power of the place and it was intoxicating. I had a problem.
>
> There is a path that circles the Parliamentary precinct and makes its way to the Supreme Court of Canada building. I walked around that path, including the Court, three times that night, praying that the power of the place would not draw me in. I didn't return to my hotel room until I felt a sense of peace.[197]

Politics is supposed to be about people, and governance can be about serving people or about wielding power over them. Surprisingly, the two can coexist. I know Members of Parliament who delight in serving their constituents. The seduction of power, however, particularly the importance of winning to hold on to power, may interfere with a servant's heart.

Even our developing *thick* faith can have *thin* spots. In those moments, we need help. Sometimes we catch ourselves. Other times, we need the support of others.

I think that's why Paul told Timothy to pray for people who hold political power. And I think that underlies Peter telling us to honour the emperor. More than submission, we honour the emperor (empress, king,

---

[197] Hutchinson, *Under Siege*, 207.

queen, president, prime minister, or anyone in the vocation of politics) by praying for him or her.

On one occasion, I attended a luncheon where Members of Parliament, senators, and diplomats were present. Hosted by a Christian organization, it was understood there would be a prayer prior to the meal.

An opposition MP had been invited to pray, and his prayer moved me to the core of my being. His respectful, conversational style revealed that he had a mature prayer life. The part of his prayer that was for Canada's government, notably the Prime Minister, evidenced that this MP prayed regularly in the spirit of Paul's letter to Timothy and Peter's injunction to the Church. There was no animosity or negativity. This man had a clear grasp of love for his political enemy (Matthew 5:43–48), expressed a biblical understanding of submission to authority (1 Peter 2:13–17), and evidenced humility before God in his prayer (1 Timothy 2:1–3).

That is where our engagement as Christian citizens in the world of politics begins: prayer. Humble submission before God enables us to understand the place of Caesar, and our role in citizenship, so that we might rightfully render to each that which belongs to them, as well as to keep our own hearts from being stained by serving a political master ahead of our divine Master.

In his book *In the Name of Jesus*, Dutch Catholic priest, theologian, and author Henri Nouwen wrote,

> One of the greatest ironies of the history of Christianity is that its leaders constantly gave in to the temptation of power—political power, military power, economic power, or moral and spiritual power—even though they continued to speak in the name of Jesus, who did not cling to his divine power but emptied himself and became as we are. The temptation to consider power an apt instrument for the proclamation of the Gospel is the greatest of all.[198]

---

[198] Henri Nouwen, *In the Name of Jesus: Reflections on Christian Leadership* (New York, NY: The Crossroad Publishing Company, 1989), 76.

It's dangerous to think we can use power to impose our understanding of God's will on other people.

Jesus and Paul engaged the power dynamic of first-century politics through submission to the authority of the state and state representatives.

Following His arrest, Jesus stood silent before the Roman governor of Judaea, Pontius Pilate, until Pilate asked,

> "You will not speak to me? Do you not know that I have authority to release you and authority to crucify you?"
>
> Jesus answered him, "You would have no authority over me at all unless it had been given you from above."
>
> —John 19:10–11

Paul summarizes what happened next in his letter to the Philippians.

> …Christ Jesus, who, though he was in the form of God, did not count equality with God a thing to be grasped, but emptied himself, by taking the form of a servant, being born in the likeness of men. And being found in human form, he humbled himself by becoming obedient to the point of death, even death on a cross.
>
> —Philippians 2:5–8

Jesus submitted to the authority of the state.

Paul had one advantage over Jesus. Jesus was a Jew from Nazareth, without rights of citizenship in the Roman Empire. Paul was a citizen. Jailed in Jerusalem. Tried by the Jewish council and arrested by the Romans, Paul appealed for state protection based on his citizenship. Subsequently, Paul languished in prison in Caesarea for two years awaiting a decision from his trial before Felix, a successor governor of Judaea (Acts 24). When a new governor, Porcius Festus, was appointed, Paul was heard out and offered a new trial, to be held in Jerusalem. Paul responded that his citizenship required his trial be held before a Roman tribunal. He appealed to be tried by Caesar (Acts 25:6–12).

Paul submitted to the authority of the state.

THE CHURCH, POLITICS

Those of us who live in a democracy have citizenship opportunities not available to those who live under religious or secular totalitarian regimes, such as the first-century Roman Empire or twenty-first-century nations like Iran, where Islam is the state religion, or communist countries like China or North Korea, which are atheist. Even in restrictive Christian nations, however, Christians can and do pray as Christians did in the first century, instructed by New Testament words written for a persecuted Church.

For the Christian citizen, the next step in political involvement is *informed* prayer. The next chapter will be about Christian citizenship and the media, but for now let's discuss a few points about being informed so we may pray with knowledge and wisdom.

One of the things I enjoy when reading Paul's letters is his specific prayers and directed comments for Christians in different cities to stay on the Way. Paul was knowledgeable of the situation in each community for which he was praying, and to which he was writing.

How did Paul know what was going on and the matters for which people required prayer? There was no internet, so no social media posts. The printing press had not yet been invented, so no daily newspapers. Paul had friends in the various Church communities, and friends who travelled between him and them as messengers.

Today, we have rapid communications, in addition to friends living in different parts of the world and friends travelling to visit different parts of the global Church. Wise use of that communication can inform our prayers for government leaders in our own nation and in other nations. The next chapter will review the importance of reliable information, but for now let me suggest what Lewis referred to as Prudence.[199] Common sense. Seek out informational sources. All media demonstrates a measure of bias, but some are more biased than others. Ween the information out of the source without necessarily accepting all the content and commentary as accurate reporting.

A general knowledge of political matters will help guide prayer and inform about specific issues on which you might desire, or feel compelled, to engage. In Canada, I have consistently had the advantage of

---

199 See Chapter Eleven: The Church, Public Engagement.

available local media, such as a neighbourhood newspaper or website in addition to chatting with my neighbours, and ready access to municipal and national media.

Be wary of social media feeds (particularly partisan feeds) and alt-media websites that interpret (or reinterpret) information to fit a partisan or extreme (left or right) position, engage in conspiracy theories, and/or publish unsupported information.

Being informed about neighbourhood issues, municipal issues, provincial issues, national issues, and international issues is easier, and more important, than some might think.

If I don't know my neighbours concerns, how can I pray intelligently for them? Or assess whether there is something I might be challenged to do to help address those concerns?

Municipal government touches our lives daily. Water supply, new housing locations, road maintenance, garbage collection, on-street parking… these, among others, are matters of municipal concern.

Canada's constitution gives significant authority to provincial governments, including to establish and regulate municipal governments and school boards. When the country that is now Canada was being negotiated, the various colonies wanted to keep key government powers with which they had been functioning, so the constitution was set up with the provinces keeping those powers and the federal government being assigned powers that would help the provinces succeed individually and together as part of Confederation. Most of the broad federal powers are in regard to matters that cross provincial boundaries.[200]

Before we progress from informed prayer, a form of action in itself, to informed participative action, it's helpful to be informed about what's going on in the *polis*, the body of citizens.

As we enter the public square informed about government and government activity, it's also helpful to have an informed theological opinion about *the things that are Caesar's* to help shape our active participation. The Bible might not tell us what person or party to vote for, but it does have some things to say about the interaction between Church and state.

---

200 Hutchinson, *Under Siege*, 12–13.

For good reason, the public square is also referred to as the public sphere. The public square refers to that space open to the public that is often found near the buildings that house municipal governments or provincial/state/federal legislatures. It is the space where opinions are expressed in support of or opposition to government, and new policy ideas are often introduced. Where no free public square exists, the space is often created in times of protest by occupying a street, intersection, or other open area that can accommodate a large gathering of citizens—or memorably in China on June 5, 1989, just one protester, often simply called "Tank Man," in Beijing's Tiananmen Square, who stood alone, blocking the progress of tanks sent to disperse protestors demonstrating for democracy.

The reason the public square is also referred to as the public sphere is a theological one, most often associated with Abraham Kuyper. Kuyper was a Dutch clergyman, journalist, theologian, and politician who served as Prime Minister of the Netherlands from 1901 to 1905.

> Kuyper promoted "principled pluralism,"[201] the idea that multiple religious expressions or worldviews, including humanism, could peacefully and respectfully coexist and participate equally in the culture and politics of the nation, including running their own schools and teaching from their particular religious perspective. As a neo-Calvinist, Kuyper promoted the idea that God is part of every aspect of everyday of life and that government has the responsibility to act in the best interests of all citizens, not just a preferred majority religious community. The concept of sphere theology was important to this understanding and expression. Rather than rights originating with the individual citizen or the state, various elements of society were seen to be sovereign in their own sphere: family, education, church, and state. In Kuyper's theology, there were clear divisions of responsibility between each sphere, with

---

201 Jonathan Chaplin, "The Point of Kuyperian Pluralism." *Comment Magazine*, November 1, 2013, https://www.cardus.ca/comment/article/4069/the-point-of-kuyperian-pluralism, accessed May 24, 2019.

each sphere answerable to God, and the spheres overlapped in the life of the citizen.[202]

Sphere theology regards the Church and the state as being two separate but overlapping spheres, or kingdoms, in the life of the citizen. The things that are God's are rendered to Him in the kingdom of God. Although God's rule is over all, God's provision for the kingdom of the emperor, or Caesar in first-century Judaea, meant that within the state we render the things that are Caesar's. The state is responsible to look out for the best interests of all citizens, not just those in the Church. As previously noted, the sphere of the state functions differently in different nations.

When we participate in the public sphere on matters of public policy, it is important that our contribution be informed by our lives in the sphere of the Church, as well as the spheres of family, education, etc. There are various opinions on what Church participation will look like in the public sphere. Some Christians and Christian communities form an enclave, almost entirely disengaged from the public sphere. Others have a long history of public sphere participation, including endeavours to influence governance and public policy.

In *Politics Under God*, Canadian political science professor and author John H. Redekop presented this biblically based, practical approach to citizenship:

> Christian citizenship is part of Christian discipleship. It is part of living consistently, responsibly, and obediently in a sinful society. While discipleship must never be fused, or confused, with good citizenship, it certainly should transform it just as much as it transforms all other aspects and dimensions of living. The ethical guidelines in our citizenship activities are exactly the same as for all other arenas of our involvement, including business, education, management, labor unions, the various professions, farming, and any other honourable pursuit undertaken by Christians. In politics, as in all other areas of life, Christians practice loving servanthood and, having

---

[202] Hutchinson, *Under Siege*, 172.

decided to get involved, do so only to the extent that Christian discipleship permits. [203]

Some ways Christians might exercise our citizenship in the public sphere include:

- Follow the work of trusted Christian organizations already active on public policy.
    - These organizations will usually have a developed biblical rationale posted on their website for each area of public policy on which they are engaged.
    - You may decide to subscribe to their publications or support their work through prayer and/or financially.
- Vote, from an informed perspective, on the issues that are important to you and the Church.
    - Don't just follow the herd in partisan alignment.
    - Assess the issues and candidates from the perspective of your faith beliefs and what is best for the good of others (most political parties and politicians now post their platform online; visit the website and inform yourself).
- Share your views with elected representatives.
    - Old-school letters, phone calls, in-person visits, and email are most effective.
    - Offer supportive encouragement and constructive criticism, as appropriate.
    - Try not to be the constant complainer.
    - Build relationships over coffee, or by attending community events where you can introduce yourself.
- Join one or more organizations that represent your faith-informed perspective on the issues and/or in the way they engage the political process.
- Join a political party and/or support a worthwhile candidate.
    - Volunteer for a candidate you support.

---

[203] John H. Redekop, *Politics Under God* (Waterloo, ON: Herald Press, 2007), 34.

- Join a local political association and get involved in shaping policy.
- Become a candidate.

Inevitably, when consideration of political involvement is being discussed, the question of civil disobedience arises. One example is found in the earlier example of Tank Man (his name is not, to my knowledge, publicly known) and the 1989 democracy demonstration in China.

Because civil disobedience is a significant step to take, with inherent risks due to confrontation with the state, I dedicated detailed comments to it in *Under Siege*:

> At this point, I think it's appropriate to reflect on some basic principles of civil disobedience. Civil disobedience is generally considered to be the publicly expressed refusal to obey certain laws, regulations, or commands of the government in order to draw attention and seek change to government policy that is considered morally offensive. It is not usually a rejection of the political system as a whole.
>
> The biblical principle of submission to government authorities is repeatedly stated in the New Testament (Matthew 22:20–22, Romans 13:1–7, Titus 3:1, 1 Peter 2:13–14). It is reflected in Western democracy's expectation that citizens will generally adhere to the laws of the land—from traffic laws to the prohibition on taking the life of another person. This social contract is crucial for us to live together as a society.
>
> But what if laws are inherently evil or harmful to our common good? And how does one assess whether laws are good or evil?
>
> For Christians in Canada, our first public effort in dealing with a harmful law is to seek to amend or replace it using democratic means. Similarly, we approach unjust laws in other nations first through diplomatic means.
>
> Civil disobedience may be justified when all other peaceful options have been tried, and failed.

A prominent American example of twentieth-century civil disobedience led by a Christian pastor stands out. Martin Luther King Jr. led non-authorized marches and other acts of civil disobedience in pursuit of change to American laws that discriminated against black Americans. King was imprisoned for his efforts and had known that was a possibility before his first engagement. He led a massive march and rally in Washington, D.C. which ultimately resulted in passage of the U.S. *Civil Rights Act of 1968*, which became law just days after his assassination. He knew the risks. He pursued the goal.

On what basis did this Christian leader, who had an earned doctorate in Christian theology, make the decision to break the law in the ways he did?

There is a biblical basis for using civil disobedience, particularly to oppose policies that dehumanize, oppress, or brutalize people. Here are some examples of civil disobedience found in Scripture:

- the Hebrew midwives saved the lives of Hebrew boys whom Pharaoh had ordered to be put to death at birth (Exodus 1:15–22, the story of Moses' birth);
- Shadrach, Meshach, and Abednego refused to obey Nebuchadnezzar's law requiring all citizens to worship a golden statue (Daniel 3, the fiery furnace story);
- Daniel, one of three presidents in Babylon, refused to pray only to King Darius for a period of thirty days (Daniel 6, the lion's den story);
- the wise men disobeyed Herod's directive to return and tell him where Jesus was born, having had it revealed to them that Herod intended to kill the child (Matthew 2:1–12); and
- the story of the Good Samaritan (Luke 10:25–37), in which Jesus endorsed breaking the religious law to help someone in dire need.

John H. Redekop identifies seven considerations for a Christian community before engaging in civil disobedience. I pose them here as questions:

1. Has the religious community made a careful and balanced assessment of the situation, including the risks of potential harm that might result from the civil disobedience?
2. Is what's at stake of great moral seriousness?
3. Has a specific goal been clearly identified that is indisputably of benefit to the common good?
4. Have all other reasonable steps been exhausted?
5. Will the behaviour planned to challenge the policy in question still demonstrate a general respect for government and the principles of lawful behaviour?
6. Will only suitable means, that make sense to non-sympathetic observers, be used?
7. Are participants prepared to accept the consequences for breaking the law that may be imposed as a result of their civil disobedience?[204]

These questions address the situation in which Dr. King accepted the responsibility and risks of becoming leader of a movement.

Two well-known first-century Christian leaders engaged in principled civil disobedience. When ordered to stop teaching about Jesus, Peter and John stated, *"We must obey God rather than men"* (Acts 5:29). This was not a general statement authorizing Christians to engage in civil disobedience when preaching is restricted by government. It was the resolution of a genuine dilemma between obedience to God for the good of others and obedience to authorities. These men were

---

[204] John H. Redekop, "Christians and Civil Disobedience: A Background Paper by the Religious Liberty Commission of The Evangelical Fellowship of Canada," Revised August 2001. See also: Redekop, *Politics Under God*, Chapter Eleven.

numbered among the disciples when Jesus told them to be His witnesses in Jerusalem (Acts 1:8). They had been in prison for doing so and were prepared to go back in order to obey Jesus' directive to them.

Civil disobedience usually takes one of two peaceful forms. Direct civil disobedience is an actual violation of an offending law, usually to bring it to consideration by the public, government, and the courts. Indirect civil disobedience is an act, such as a rally or a march that may break traffic laws or municipal permit bylaws, intended to draw attention to the offending law.[205]

As Christians, our participation in politics starts and ends with prayer. Pray for government officials. Pray about our participation. Pray as we participate. And then pray for government officials, that those in positions of authority would look out for the best interests of all citizens, including Christian citizens.

One of the most influential world leaders of our lifetime in the area of politics is non-partisan. She is a diminutive woman who is unabashedly Christian in her approach to life, service, and politics.

When Elizabeth Windsor's father died unexpectedly while she was in Kenya, Princess Elizabeth became Queen of the United Kingdom, and of Canada among other Commonwealth realms. Queen Elizabeth II is not required to care for the poor, be attentive to strangers, or speak publicly about her belief in Jesus Christ, but she does. From her earliest radio broadcast on her twenty-first birthday in 1947,[206] in her annual Christmas addresses over the last six decades, and at other times, Elizabeth II has been very public that "I know how much I rely on my faith to guide me through the good times and the bad… I draw strength from the message of hope in the Christian gospel."[207]

In 1986, the Queen said:

---

[205] Hutchinson, *Under Siege*, 201–203.
[206] Mark Greene and Catherine Butcher, *The Servant Queen and the King She Serves, with a Foreword by Her Majesty Queen Elizabeth II* (London, UK: Bible Society, HOPE, LICC, 2016), 12.
[207] Ibid., 6.

His (Jesus') life thus began in humble surroundings, in fact in a stable, but he was to have a profound influence on the course of history, and on the lives of generations of his followers. You don't have to be rich or powerful in order to change things for the better and each of us in our own way can make a contribution.[208]

We cannot all be a monarch, with the attendant privileges and responsibilities, but we can influence the realm we touch, whether great or small.

The Queen rarely misses church on Sunday. Commenting on world happenings and personal difficulties she experienced in 1992, Her Majesty expressed gratitude for "all those whose prayers—fervent, I hope, but not too frequent—have sustained me."[209] On other occasions she has also mentioned her prayers for those whom she serves as Queen, notably in many of her annual Christmas addresses. About that 1992 speech, one of the Queen's biographers writes,

> In a secular age, it is perhaps surprising to hear a leading international figure who is not a member of the clergy talk of prayer in the middle of a public speech. The Queen didn't have to do so. She chose to do so.[210]

In 2016, for her ninetieth birthday, the United Kingdom's longest-serving monarch wrote, "I have been—and remain—very grateful to you for your prayers and to God for His steadfast love."[211]

Prayer does make a difference.

For most Christians, we are challenged in our earthly citizenship to move from prayer to participatory action in the political process, action which covers the range from informed voting to governance as an elected officeholder. Let us do so with upward-mindedness, forward-thinking,

---

208 Ibid., 26.
209 Ibid., 56.
210 Ibid., 56.
211 Ibid., Foreword by Her Majesty Queen Elizabeth II.

and the well-being of all in mind, for in their well-being we will find our well-being (Jeremiah 29:4–7).

Three Takeaways

- Politicians are people, *imago Dei* like you and me, and the healthy participation of people makes politics work.
- Pray for our political leaders; federal, provincial (or state), and municipal.
- Civil obedience is the first option for the Christian citizen. Civil disobedience is the last.

CHAPTER THIRTEEN

THE CHURCH, MEDIA

Again he began to teach beside the sea. And a very large crowd gathered about him, so that he got into a boat and sat in it on the sea, and the whole crowd was beside the sea on the land. And he was teaching them many things in parables, and in his teaching he said to them: "Listen! Behold, a sower went out to sow. And as he sowed, some seed fell along the path, and the birds came and devoured it. Other seed fell on rocky ground, where it did not have much soil, and immediately it sprang up, since it had no depth of soil. And when the sun rose, it was scorched, and since it had no root, it withered away. Other seed fell among thorns, and the thorns grew up and choked it, and it yielded no grain. And other seeds fell into good soil and produced grain, growing up and increasing and yielding thirtyfold and sixtyfold and a hundredfold."
—Mark 4:1–8

A soft answer turns away wrath, but a harsh word stirs up anger.
—Proverbs 15:1

If one gives an answer before he hears [listens], it is his folly and shame.
—Proverbs 18:13

THERE ARE MULTIPLE SIDES TO CHRISTIAN CITIZENSHIP AND MEDIA (IN WHICH I include social media). What media do you take in? What media do you rebroadcast? What do you share as a participant in media? How do you assess the accuracy of what you receive and what you personally broadcast?

Growing up, we frequently had dinner on TV trays while watching the six o'clock news. Mum was parenting three kids and working full-time. By the time dinner was prepared, it might be near six. In our household, it was important to understand the news of our city, province, nation, and the world, particularly the big neighbour to our south that had regular coverage but wasn't consigned to the world news segment of the broadcast. We also had a newspaper subscription.

As I got older, I added the ten o'clock news to my nightly viewing. On Fridays and Saturdays, I watched the eleven o'clock news on a different network. The hosts of these later broadcasts often concluded by saying goodnight. I developed the habit of returning the greeting. "Good night, Uncle Knowlty." "Good night, Lloyd." I still do, although sometimes with additional comments on the quality of the newscast. I let them know when their commentary didn't match news clip content, along with other journalistic failures or successes. They don't hear my comments, so these are one-sided conversations.

Spending summer vacations with my dad, there were two daily must-watch TV shows: *Sesame Street*,[212] which helped with my rudimentary Spanish, and the six o'clock news in English.

Today I check several news sources. Five newspaper apps. A Twitter feed that allows me to intentionally follow select media, reputable organizations, bloggers, social media sites, and individuals. I go beyond the headlines to scan or read the content. Headlines and content don't always line up. Most days I still watch the six o'clock and ten o'clock news on TV.

Sowing seed (Matthew 13:3–9; Mark 4:1–8; Luke 8:4–8) isn't just about sharing the Scriptures or planting literal seeds in the ground with the intent of harvesting a crop, it's also about our use of media.[213] Prudence (common sense) is required in our assessment of the seeds we allow

---

212 *Sesame Street*. Created by Joan Ganz Cooney and Lloyd Morrisett, produced by Sesame Workshop (previously known as Children's Television Workshop). First episode aired November 10, 1969. An educational children's television series that combines live action, sketch comedy, animation, and puppetry. Muppets (puppets) designed by Jim Henson.
213 Contributor Lorna Dueck shares a similar thought in: Georgialee Lang, ed., *Faith, Life and Leadership: 8 Canadian Women Tell Their Stories* (Belleville, ON: Castle Quay Books, 2017), 20.

to be sown into us, because they take root and grow. Prudence is also required for the seeds we sow. Take the time to think about what you are doing, and what is likely to come of it.[214] This is particularly true in the current era in which almost anyone can blog, meme, or share, but seemingly few fact-check.

In the story Jesus told, using the available media of the day, a sower was spreading seed by hand, a small quantity at a time, across a large area over a long period of time. In regard to media in the twenty-first century, we are not hand-seeders but broadcast-spreaders covering vast territory in an instant. Other broadcast-spreaders share with us and we with them, and they with others, and so on.

As English Anglican priest and theologian John Stott stated in the first line of the preface to Malcom Muggeridge's book *Christ and the Media*, "The influence of the mass media upon us all is continuous, insistent and pervasive."[215] In the body of the text, Muggeridge, an English journalist, augments Stott's comment, stating,

> This influence, I should add, is, in my opinion, largely exerted irresponsibly, arbitrarily, and without reference to any moral or intellectual, still less spiritual, guidelines whatsoever...
>
> The ostensibly serious offerings of the media, on the other hand, represent a different menace precisely because they are liable to pass for being objective and authentic... This applies especially to news and so-called documentaries, both of which are regarded as factual, but which, in practice, are processed along with everything else in the media's fantasy-machine. Thus news becomes, not so much what has happened, as what can be seen as happening, or seems to have happened. As for documentaries, anyone who has worked on them, as I have extensively, knows that the element of simulation in them has

---

214 Lewis, *Mere Christianity*, 70.
215 Malcolm Muggeridge, *Christ and the Media* (Grand Rapids, MI: William B. Eerdmans Publishing Company, 1977), 3. The book is an edited version of lectures given in the 1976 London Lectures in Contemporary Christianity, sponsored by the Langham Trust. Muggeridge began his career in media in 1930, moving from print to television in the mid-1950s.

always been considerable, and has only increased as making and directing them has become more sophisticated and technically developed.²¹⁶

Three decades later, in his 2009 book *Through a Lens Darkly*, a study of Canadian news media treatment of evangelical Christians based on a review of the framing for news stories between 1994 and 2005, associate professor David Haskell of Wilfred Laurier University makes a similar point, and extends the point to note the role of the audience:

> The greatest problem with news is not that journalists are influenced by their perceptions; the greatest problem is that news audiences do not realize journalists are influenced by their perceptions.²¹⁷

Mass media, of course, now includes mainstream media and social media, among other types. Yes, prudence, common sense, and even diligence is required. We are not passive recipients of the seeds planted by media.

Christians are needed who will hold fast to truth in themselves and in media representations. Christian media representation takes place in mainstream media, Christian media, social media (Facebook, Twitter, Instagram, etc.), blogging, etc. Christians active in media include professional journalists as well as amateurs like you and me. We must be mindful of the biases in the media we receive, and our own biases in what we produce and share—the seeds sown into us, and the seeds we sow.

Why is it important to be mindful of biases in presentation? We are ambassadors for Jesus (2 Corinthians 5:20). We don't want to become

---

216 Ibid., 23, 61–62. Muggeridge compares reality with fantasy throughout the text, noting the fantastical nature of the media presenting a perspective informed by ideas about what is progressive, and shaping opinion rather than providing objective presentation. Reality, he reminds us, is found in Christ and living life with Christ kept first in mind and action.

217 David M. Haskell, *Through a Lens Darkly: How the News Media Perceive and Portray Evangelicals* (Toronto, ON: Clements Academic, 2009), 211.

the story that betrays that role. Barry McLoughlin has said, "Hypocrisy in religion is the low hanging fruit of the media."[218] It's up to us not to provide that low-hanging fruit.

Here are a few prudent thoughts for sorting out the media we receive.

- Who is the messenger? What is their bias?
    - News media: tends to have a conformist-collectivist mindset that is informed by and informs societal biases.[219] News media may conform to fit/counter its immediate media culture (e.g. conservative media outlet in a progressive/liberal society).
    - Partisan media: consistently supports a political position and frames stories to agree with that position.
    - Religious media: bias is informed by religious perspective and situations. It may be reliable (objective reports) or tainted (e.g. partisan in disposition, fundraising may be dependent on the perspective reported, may fail to fact-check).
    - Alt-media: has a strong bias to a particular issue or extreme position from which it frames stories (often politically extreme, left or right).
    - Academic media: likely bias related to an academic background/specialty.
    - Amateur media: likely bias based on personal interests/views, and they may or may not fact-check.
- For whom is the message prepared?
    - News media, for a general audience.
    - Partisan, for a political audience.
    - Religious, often for a supportive religious audience.

---

218 Barry J. McLoughlin, statement made during "Encountering the Media: A Seminar by McLoughlin Media," which I attended in Ottawa, Canada, August 27–29, 2008. The seminar resource book was Barry J. McLoughlin, *Encountering the Media: Media Strategies and Techniques* (Ottawa, ON: McLoughlin Multi-Media Strategies, 2005).
219 Muggeridge, *Christ and the Media*, 52.

- Alt-media, for an audience prone to agreement with an extreme position.
- Academic, for a general/academic/other specific audience.
- Amateur, for a general or networked audience, most of whom agree with the message.
- How reliable is the messenger?
  - Consider their track record.
  - Consider the reliability of the organization sharing the information.
  - Do a simple search of the author and the media outlet. The reliability of whatever information they share about themselves can usually be easily assessed by consideration of other sources.
- How readily can the message be fact-checked or verified by other sources?
  - Is the source of statistics or statements in a meme or article stated and accessible?
  - Is the information in alignment with other reliable sources?
- How current is the information?
  - Specific information, such as persecution alerts or political statements, may be time-sensitive and potentially overtaken by subsequent events.
  - General information can be relevant for an extended period of time depending on the content and its intended purpose or use.

The answer to those questions may also help determine whether you should share the information. My heart sinks when I see a comment on social media informing the original Christian poster that the information is no longer relevant (e.g. that report is from four years ago) or is verifiably tainted in some other way (e.g. that false story has been circulating on the internet for years, or those statistics are made up, etc.). We all make mistakes, but Christians are encouraged to make the effort to avoid the *low-hanging fruit*.

In addition to being truthful, are we being Christ-like in the media seeds we plant?

Why are you sharing the message? What do you desire to accomplish? What is the issue that needs to be addressed? What's the goal? Who is your audience? Who else will see your message?

Remember, we're sowing seeds without knowing exactly where or how they will grow. Let's make them good seeds.

The good seed concept also applies if we become the subject of media stories, and media wants to hear our message.

I once had a boss who said, "No publicity is bad publicity, as long as they remember your name." Perhaps, but only as long as they don't associate your name in a negative way.

If you end up on the receiving end of reporters' phone calls and emails, or unexpectedly see your name in media reports, try not to panic. Keep breathing. Maintain your integrity. Prepare yourself.

Is it a legal matter? I suggest calling a lawyer. It's true that anything you say may be used against you in a court of law. It may also be used against you in the court of public opinion. (Keep breathing.)

In the first century, Paul was charged with a crime. He did the equivalent of calling a lawyer when he appealed to have his case heard before Caesar (Acts 25:10–12).

If confronted by media, not responding may be better than saying, "No comment." Other ways of truthfully saying nothing while you sort out what's going on are statements such as,

- "I didn't expect you (or your question). I'll have to take some time to think about a response."
- "I may not be the person to answer that. Do you have contact information?"

There is no requirement to answer questions from the media, any media, even when they say "The public has a right to know." Think about it. There is no such right.

Jesus didn't have to contend with journalists or bloggers in his day, but we can learn from him on this point. In the last chapter, we considered briefly Jesus' appearance before Pontius Pilate. Let's revisit that portion of their time together:

> *He entered his headquarters again and said to Jesus, "Where are you from?" But Jesus gave him no answer. So Pilate said to him, "You will not speak to me? Do you not know that I have authority to release you and authority to crucify you?"*
>
> *Jesus answered him, "You would have no authority over me at all unless it had been given you from above. Therefore he who delivered me over to you has the greater sin."*
>
> —John 19:9–11

Notice that Pilate knew the answer to the question on which Jesus remained silent.

What do you think the typical person would have said if Caesar's representative had asked, "Where are you from?" Jesus chose silence. Pilate pushed back with a threat that essentially declared "I have a right to know." Jesus replied truthfully, but He didn't answer the question. He said what He considered important, but it wasn't an answer to the *yes* or *no* question Pilate had asked. Instead Pilate received a seed about the kingdom of God.

Even though we might have friendly one-sided conversations with mainstream media personalities during a newscast, talking with them in person may or may not be the time to have an actual conversation, depending on why they want to talk. If it's someone from Christian media, the conversation may unfold differently than if it's someone from mainstream media, or a blogger hoping to write a story that goes viral.

If the media request is from an "unfriendly," what can we learn from Jesus about how to respond?

First, silence is an option.

Second, if you're going to engage, know your goal and develop a route to get there.

When Jesus was first taken to Pilate, the allegation was that Jesus claimed to be a king, which would have made him a treasonous competitor to Caesar. Treason warranted the death penalty. Jesus told the truth, asked questions to challenge Pilate's perspective, and planted a seed: *"My kingdom is not of this world"* (John 18:36). Jesus knew He was headed to his death, and He was still planting seeds of the Gospel.

In the end, the charge Pilate nailed on the cross above Jesus' head was "Jesus of Nazareth, King of the Jews." He posted the sign in Aramaic, Greek, and Latin, the languages of the common person, business leaders, and governing authority in Jerusalem (John 19:16–22).

Before we continue with the third and fourth possible responses to "unfriendly" media requests, here's another example of Jesus being questioned/challenged. He knew his goal and had a route to get to it that followed truthful talking points to the questions posed, although not necessarily answers to the questions. In Matthew 4, we read the story of Jesus' temptations in the wilderness.

> *And the tempter came and said to him, "If you are the Son of God, command these stones to become loaves of bread." But he answered, "It is written, 'Man shall not live by bread alone, but by every word that comes from the mouth of God.'"*
>
> — Matthew 4:3–4 (Jesus quoting from Deuteronomy 8:3)

Notice that Jesus did not say He wouldn't turn the stones into bread. Jesus made His statement, a brief talking point, to refute the tempter's challenge to His character.

> *Then the devil took him to the holy city and set him on the pinnacle of the temple and said to him, "If you are the Son of God, throw yourself down, for it is written, 'He will command his angels concerning you,' and 'On their hands they will bear you up, lest you strike your foot against a stone.'"*

> *Jesus said to him, "Again it is written, 'You shall not put the Lord your God to the test.'"*
>
> —Matthew 4:5–7
> (the devil quoting from Psalm 91:11–12
> and the Jesus quoting from Deuteronomy 6:16)

The devil tries to twist God's words, as reporters seem prone to do with those who speak with them, but Jesus knows His talking point. Again, it's not a direct answer to the challenge but the truth, and on point:

> *Again, the devil took him to a very high mountain and showed him all the kingdoms of the world and their glory. And he said to him, "All these I will give you, if you will fall down and worship me."*
>
> *Then Jesus said to him, "Be gone, Satan! For it is written, 'You shall worship the Lord your God and him only shall you serve.'"*
>
> —Matthew 4:8–10 (Jesus quoting from Deuteronomy 6:13)

Again, Jesus responds to Satan's challenge. A clear talking point, an on-point statement, but not a direct answer.

> *Then the devil left him, and behold, angels came and were ministering to him.*
>
> —Matthew 4:11

So what's a talking point? A talking point is a positive statement that expresses the essence of the message one desires to convey. It's brief and memorable. The words are strong and easy to understand. In media terms, it's a soundbite. If you have a story to back up your talking point, you save it for a setting in which you can control the message that will be relayed in the media, perhaps an opinion piece written by you for the local newspaper or a live or live-to-tape broadcast or podcast, or your own blog—but it won't be shared where, as Muggeridge said, it can be "processed along with everything else in the media's fantasy-machine."[220]

---

[220] Muggeridge, *Christ and the Media*, 61.

Haskell notes research from American sociologist Steven Clayman which shows that reporters select quotes and soundbites for their stories based on three things: the narrative relevance of the statement to fit with the story they're telling, the sensational nature of the statement, and the simplicity with which the statement can be taken from a longer interview and dropped into a shorter news report.[221]

Reporters have a bias. When you have a message that you want communicated in your words and from your perspective, use talking points.

In putting together messaging language for media (or for public engagement or communicating on political issues), consider how Jesus and first-century Church leaders were strategic and purposeful in their communication to make it relevant to their audience.

American sociologist and pastor Tony Campolo and American professor of media and communications Mary Albert Darling summarize that idea in one short sentence in their book *Connecting Like Jesus*: "Jesus and the early Christ-followers spoke differently to different audiences."[222] [223]

Here's how I unpacked that concept in *Under Siege*:

> To a faithful and expectant Jewish people, Jesus delivered a message of hope and words that clarified their expectations. To fishermen, He spoke of becoming fishers of men (Matthew 4:19). To farmers, He spoke of seedtime and the harvest (Mark 4:1–9).
>
> To the religious leaders of Jesus' day, Jesus often delivered a challenge to be faithful to God, God's revelation, and God's people rather than the rules and regulations of a religion that had created hurdles on the path of those seeking to follow God. In fact, the religious leaders were the only people Jesus ever referred to with harsh words: "hypocrites," "blind guides," "whitewashed tombs," and a "brood of vipers"

---

221 Haskel, *Through a Lens Darkly*, 97.
222 Tony Campolo and Mary Albert Darling, *Connecting Like Jesus: Practices for Healing, Teaching, and Preaching* (San Francisco, CA: Jossey-Bass, 2010), 172–173.
223 Generally in regard to cross-cultural communication as Western Christians in Western culture, see: Lesslie Newbigin, *Foolishness to the Greeks: The Gospel and Western Culture* (Grand Rapids, MI: Eerdmans, 1988).

(Matthew 23:13–33). It was also in regard to their decision to permit business in the prayer court of the temple that Jesus gave His lone public demonstration of physically aggressive behaviour, turning over tables of commerce, with none of that force directed toward people (Mark 11:15–19).

To the political masters of Rome, and their courts of law, Jesus and His disciples were consistently respectful. Respect, however, does not require compromise of one's faith to the arena of political or public opinion.

In Athens, Paul spoke to academics and philosophers in a way that appealed to their intellect, quoting from one of their own well-known philosophers and a Greek poet to make his point about Jesus (Acts 17:16–34).[224]

Even with easily understood talking points, there is no guarantee the story that gets written won't be framed in a contrary way.

Third on the list of possible responses to a media inquiry, and perhaps most importantly, we can pray. There is no prohibition on seeking divine guidance. *Selah*... pause and reflect.[225] Remember when the crowd brought a woman caught in adultery and demanded to know what Jesus had to say about her punishment? *Selah*. He paused and reflected, and perhaps He prayed, before He answered (John 8:1–11).

Neither reporters nor social media adversaries are Satan incarnate, whether or not it seems like they're trying to undermine you, me, or Christ's work.

For we do not wrestle against flesh and blood, but against the rulers, against the authorities, against the cosmic powers over this present darkness, against the spiritual forces of evil in the heavenly places.
—Ephesians 6:12

---

[224] Hutchinson, *Under Siege*, 227–228.
[225] James Strong, *Strong's Exhaustive Concordance, Hebrew and Chaldee Dictionary*, #5542 (*celah*, suspension [of music], i.e. pause), #5541 (*calah*, to hang up, i.e. to weigh, evaluate).

Pray. Reporters may hold a different worldview. They may speak a different cultural language. They may neither understand nor like your perspective.

The media are regarded by many as authorities in our twenty-first century world. When standing before authorities, Jesus said, *"[D]o not be anxious about how you should defend yourself or what you should say, for the Holy Spirit will teach you in that very hour what you ought to say"* (Luke 12:11-12). So pray.

Fourth, and finally, remember that we are ambassadors for Jesus. We are to treat all people, including the media and those we encounter on social media, from the perspective of *imago Dei*, for we and they are made in the image of God.

Treating others the way you would like them to treat you (Matthew 7:12) is an important part of Christian media strategy, whether or not we're treated well in return. Our lives are witness seeds sown for the Gospel.

One person sowing seeds for the Gospel, and exercising influence through traditional and social media, is Canadian Lorna Dueck. Dueck has been a journalist for more than thirty years, a career that followed the simple prayer, "Lord, let me impact the media for you."[226]

Starting a school newspaper at the Winkler Bible Institute led her to an opportunity to work as a radio news announcer and later in television news in Manitoba. In 1994, Dueck moved into Christian media, invited by David Mainse to co-host *100 Huntley Street*, a national daily television ministry. Her career focus became "looking journalistically for 'the God angle.'"[227]

A leading figure in Christian media, Dueck was appointed CEO of Crossroads Global Media Group in 2016, which includes the YES TV

---

[226] *Faytene.TV*, "Media in Canada, Guest: Lorna Dueck." Faytene Grasseschi. August 4, 2019 (https://www.youtube.com/watch?v=uAGm5nKHvb4&t=1s). Unless otherwise noted, the following quotes from Lorna Dueck in this chapter come from that interview.

[227] Lang, *Faith, Life and Leadership*, 2. Dueck also tells her career story in the chapter "Communicating on a Faith Frequency."

network. She also hosts the weekly program *Context with Lorna Dueck*[228] and writes on faith and public life for *The Globe and Mail*, one of Canada's leading national newspapers.

In a 2019 interview with Faytene Grasseschi on Faytene.TV, Dueck observed the interaction between traditional media, social media, and Christians:

> Media is a very complex world. And it needs you and me… to engage it so it doesn't just go its own merry way. It has to have accountability to the citizenship.

It is important to be aware and to be involved. Dueck also commented on the danger of our absence from media participation.

> If you are a follower of Christ… and you never see yourself in media, the national conversation then unfolds that there probably is no faith in Canada, or it is marginalized, or it's not important.

In a 2012 interview with Magdalene John on *100 Huntley Street*, Dueck stated:

> The future for God in media is for the people who know Him to make themselves more accessible… We really need to be part of the fray… The people of God just have to join that high risk communication and be part of it.[229]

---

228 According to the show's website, "Context is Canada's premiere Christian voice in news and current affairs… Context's team of broadcast journalists report on complex stories and are there when major stories break… the show provides a platform for Canadian and global issues. Context's distinctive voice gives our audience a perspective they don't hear in other media" ("About," *Context with Lorna Dueck*. Date of access: August 19, 2019 [http://www.contextwithlornadueck.com/about]).

229 *100 Huntley Street*, "Finding God in the News." Magdalene John. December 1, 2012 (http://www.100huntley.com/watch?id=217815).

It's imperative that we recognize the influence media has on our own thoughts, and strategically engage in ways that recognize, as Dueck has said, that "we are stewards of the gift of the media."

Lorna Dueck has also expressed clearly the significance of being aware that we are representatives of Jesus at all times, very visibly, when we engage in the media world.

> There are many issues I would like to rant and be polemic on, there is a sarcasm and biting wit that would make for energy in a column, but I most often hit delete on these impulses because, in my mind, it is incompatible with Gospel witness.[230]

We participate in media. Let us do so wisely. We are stewards of our intake and our output. We are ambassadors for Christ, sowers of His good seed.

Three Takeaways

- Be thoughtful about the media you take in.
- Be careful about the media you put out.
- Use common sense in your ambassadorial role for Christ when dealing with reporters.

---

[230] Jennifer Neutel, "Q&A with Lorna Dueck," *Christian Courier*. April 11, 2016 (http://www.christiancourier.ca/news/entry/qa-with-lorna-dueck).

CHAPTER FOURTEEN

THE CHURCH, THE ENVIRONMENT

And God blessed them. And God said to them, "Be fruitful and multiply and fill the earth and subdue it, and have dominion over the fish of the sea and over the birds of the heavens and over every living thing that moves on the earth." And God said, "Behold, I have given you every plant yielding seed that is on the face of all the earth, and every tree with seed in its fruit. You shall have them for food. And to every beast of the earth and to every bird of the heavens and to everything that creeps on the earth, everything that has the breath of life, I have given every green plant for food."

—Genesis 1:28–30

The Lord God took the man and put him in the garden of Eden to work it and keep it.

—Genesis 2:15

BEFORE THERE WERE NATIONS, CITIES, TOWNS, VILLAGES, OR NEIGHBOURHOODS, before there were people, there was creation. Whether one accepts the Genesis account as authoritative or prefers concepts found in the theory of evolution (and its various permutations and combinations), humans were not first on the scene.

I have intentionally not addressed policy issues in this book. Some might consider the environment to be a policy issue, but I see our concern for it as a matter of citizenship and theology: the first responsibility given to humans as citizens of Earth was to be stewards of God's creation.

PART II: IN SOCIETY

In thoughts on citizenship shared through the prophet Jeremiah, God includes the instruction to plant gardens along with building houses, getting married, having children, and praying for the city on the list of activities that demonstrate seeking the well-being of the community (Jeremiah 29:4–8). The word *plant*[231] means just what you think it means. The word *garden*[232] also means just what you think it means. In addition to homeowners being able to eat the fruit of their gardens, consider the benefit that the trees and plants must have been for the *"welfare of the city"* (Jeremiah 29:7), or God would not have instructed it be done.

When I was in high school, global cooling was the climate threat to the world. Already a *Star Trek* fan, I also tuned in to *In Search Of...*, which featured *Star Trek*'s Mr. Spock, Leonard Nimoy, as host. The show explored strange and supposedly unexplainable phenomena. Just before I graduated from high school, Nimoy explored the coming ice age.[233] There was then an apparently multidecade pattern evidenced through scientific measurement that we were near the end of life as we knew it because of global cooling.

Within a decade, the language used transitioned to global warming. Decreasing polar ice and rising sea levels left a little over a decade to bring about correction before, again, we were facing an irreversible trend toward the end of life as we knew it. We were not going to make it to the second millennium. And then we did.

Not long after that, the schedule for global warming's destruction of the planet was revised. The new revision was headlined in public declarations by former U.S. Vice-President and unsuccessful presidential candidate Al Gore, reaching an apex with his film *An Inconvenient Truth* in 2006.[234]

More recently, the term *climate change* is being used. It may actually be the oldest of the three terms, first coined by scientists who were uncertain about the direction of future climate because of conflicting evidence

---

231 James Strong, *Strong's Exhaustive Concordance, Hebrew and Chaldee Dictionary*, #5193 (*nata*, to strike in; specifically to plant [figuratively or literally]).
232 Ibid., #1593 (*gannah*, a garden).
233 *In Search Of...*, "The Coming Ice Age." Season 2, Episode 23. Written by Philip Dauber. May 18, 1978.
234 *An Inconvenient Truth,* directed by David Guggenheim (Los Angeles, CA: Paramount Classics, 2006).

that supported global cooling and global warming. The key was to watch the long-term trends of climate change.[235]

The terms *climate crisis* and *climate emergency* became more prevalent following the 2015 Paris Agreement,[236] negotiated between the 196 nations represented at the twenty-first Conference of the Parties (COP 21) of the *United Nations Framework Convention on Climate Change*.

The declaration, by some, of a climate emergency has created an artificial dichotomy in discussion on the topic. One is classified either a climate emergency believer or a climate emergency sceptic. Scientists, celebrities, politicians, and Christians are divided into both camps.

What if there is another option?

In the 1980s, Gloria and I were privileged to lead camps for Indigenous children in northern British Columbia. What better place to introduce concepts of understanding and caring for "God's Wonderful Creation," as we titled one series of camps? It was a week of introducing children to critical thinking from a biblical perspective. In addition to the biblical account of creation, we considered the "faith" required to accept evolution. We also enjoyed the requisite camp activities of swimming, horseback riding, and campfires.

Does it make more sense that the universe spontaneously came into being from nothing, by chance, or by the words of the Designer? Does it make more sense that single cells developed in a myriad of directions, forming multiple plants and creatures, or that there is a Creator? Does it make more sense that science is, by its nature, quiet on the morality of caring for the environment or that God speaks to us, telling us to be stewards caring for His creation? Must science rule or is discovery compatible with revelation?

---

235 Mike Hulme, "Climate Change (Concept of)," *The International Encyclopedia of Geography*. Date of access: May 30, 2019 (https://www.academia.edu/10358797/Climate_change_concept_of). Hulme begins the article by discussing the coining of the term *climatic change* by the World Meteorological Organization in a 1966 technical report.

236 United Nations, *Paris Agreement to the United Nations Framework Convention on Climate Change*, December 12, 2015, T.I.A.S. No. 16–1104 (entered into force November 4, 2016).

Gloria and I developed the teaching materials, designing camp crafts to be an ongoing reminder of the week.

For since the creation of the world His invisible attributes, His eternal power and divine nature, have been clearly seen, being understood through what has been made...
—Romans 1:20, NASB

We get to be co-curators of God's wonderful creation (Genesis 2:15)! Indian educator and theologian Ken Gnanakan has written, "When we start our theology from creation, God's mission becomes an all-embracing mission with a concern for all of humanity as well as God's creation."[237]

A few years ago, I pulled out the camp curriculum in preparation to speak at a conference called Climate Change and Environmental Decline as a Moral Issue. My take on the topic came from the moral perspective.

While I have only skirted the edges of the science, I find that the issue is unsettled except for one key reality: climate changes. From the moral perspective, humans are unique in our capacity to enhance or destroy all of planet Earth and its inhabitants based on *our* decisions.[238]

The presence of humans has an impact on environmental decline. Think about the impact of deforestation required to accommodate ever-expanding civilization. Humans also pollute. Pollution and environmental decline have an impact on climate and on the consequences of extreme environmental events. That combination suggests to me that humans have an impact on climate change, whether direct or indirect. And humans have the moral responsibility to do something about it. But what?

My conference talk outlined the biblical basis for stewardship of God's creation, whether climate emergency believer or sceptic. At the end, a young environmentalist, wholly opposed to the industrial nature of the global economy, insisted I make the effort to learn the science. She also challenged me to open doors to get her into evangelical churches so

---

237 Ken Gnanakan, World Evangelical Alliance Theological Commission, *Responsible Stewardship of God's Creation* (Bangalore, KA: Theological Book Trust, 2004), 27.
238 Although Revelation 21 must be factored in to this particular consideration as a limitation on that capacity. And please, no predicted dates or times for the end of the world (Matthew 24:36–44; 1 Thessalonians 5:1–3; 2 Peter 3:10; Revelation 3:3).

that Christians could be convinced by the science, presumably to fall in line with those who believed as she did. I agreed to do so, provided she first get me into her climate clubs to preach the Gospel and principles of biblical stewardship for creation, to present an opportunity for others to believe as I do. No invitations were exchanged.

I don't *need* to learn the science. I do benefit from having confidence in one or more reliable sources on the science that facilitate a prudent application of the morality found in the Bible. Although the Bible makes the point on its own.

One reasoned source for information on the science associated with climate change is Katharine Hayhoe. Hayhoe has the threefold distinction of being Christian, Canadian, and a climate scientist. We might not align on everything around climate science, but we agree on Christ. I've read some of her work in *Faith Today* and in *Convivium Magazine* and found her presentation to be sensible.

Hayhoe is a good communicator. In a recent *Châtelaine* magazine article, Hayhoe used common English to debunk what she considers to be six common climate change myths (unless otherwise noted, the coming quotations are from that *Châtelaine* article).[239]

1. "It's been warmer before, so it can't be humans now." It has been warmer before. Cooler, too. But now, with more than seven and a half billion people living on the planet, we need to take human contribution into account. Twenty-first-century societies produce "massive amounts of heat-trapping gases."

2. "Scientists still aren't sure about this whole thing." The basic science about climate change is understood. The science of climate change is about factors connected to the history of acknowledged climate changes. Based on those factors, the current pattern is warming on a global scale.

3. "Canada's not big enough to make a difference." Canada's current emissions are about two percent of the global total, but emissions per Canadian are high, two and a half times that of a person in the United

---

239 Katharine Hayhoe, "6 Myths About Climate Change Debunked," *Châtelaine*. April 10, 2019 (https://www.chatelaine.com/living/climate-change-myths-debunked-by-scientist). *Châtelaine* is a Canadian magazine. I have summarized Dr. Hayhoe's comments.

Kingdom, ten times a person in Zimbabwe, and twenty times a person in Yemen.

4. "Climate change is a good thing for Canada." Climate change is a global phenomenon, already seriously and negatively affecting other nations, including harm to humans. It's not about warmer winters. As she says, "It's not about saving the planet. The planet will survive. It's about saving *us*."

On this vital point, Gnanakan agrees from the theological perspective with Hayhoe's conclusion from the science.

> Here is a sobering thought: creation can survive without humans, but *we* cannot last long without drawing from some of creation's bounties![240]

Genesis 1 makes it clear that while humans might be considered the culmination of creation, we cannot exist without all that was created before us.

5. "It's cold outside. Global warming can't be real." Hayhoe points out, "Weather is what occurs in a certain place at a certain time. Climate is the long-term average of weather over decades." The current pattern is a warming trend.

6. "Helping the environment will kill the economy." Hayhoe identifies Canada as a global leader in clean technology, well-positioned for changes in the energy sector.

I don't necessarily agree with everything Hayhoe has to say, but her presentation is reasonable and touches on the moral issue of why we should care, the very issue which is addressed by Scripture. Our choices are impacting others in a negative, even dangerous and life-threatening way.

In *God's Earthkeepers*,[241] Canadian environmental consultant William van Geest addresses answers to that moral concern from a biblical perspective.

---

240 Gnanakan, *Responsible Stewardship*, 31.
241 William van Geest, *God's Earthkeepers: Biblical Action and Reflection on the Environment* (Willowdale, ON: The Evangelical Fellowship of Canada, 1995). Updated in 2007, with the second edition available in PDF format at https://files.evangelicalfellowship.ca/si/Environment/God_s_Earthkeepers.pdf. Date of access: May 27, 2019.

1. "God loves all of creation."[242] God created the heavens and the earth, and all that exists (Genesis 1). He continues to feed the birds of the air and clothe the grass of the field (Matthew 6:26–30). David's Psalm 24 begins, *"The earth is the Lord's and the fullness thereof [and all that fills it]…"* (Psalm 24:1)

God cares. There is an inherent worth in humans as image-bearers.[243] There is also, as stated by Gnanakan, "an inherent worth in creation and not just value for the sake of human utility."[244]

2. "Creation reveals God."[245] Van Geest goes on to write, "As awesome and wonderful as the creation is, however, we don't worship it. It always points us beyond itself to the Creator."[246] Jesus came into creation and lived in the flesh to give us a life-changing revelation of God's love (John 3:16).

3. "We are an inseparable part of God's creation."[247] Humans were created from, and as part of, creation (Genesis 2:7).

4. "We have a special role and responsibility within creation."[248] We have been made in the image of God (Genesis 1:26–27) and given dominion over creation (Genesis 1:28–30) as God's image-bearers. Van Geest writes, "We reflect God's presence on the earth. Individually and collectively, we are accountable to God for what we do with and on this earth."[249] We alone have been placed in the garden to work it and keep it (Genesis 2:15).

5. "In our fall, we are alienated from creation."[250] The brokenness in relationship with God that came from the fall of Adam and Eve resulted in a changed relationship with nature (Genesis 3:17–19) and the opening for our dominion to be exercised in a manner that can be destructive.

---

242 Ibid., 5.
243 For more on this subject, see Chapter Ten.
244 Gnanakan, *Responsible Stewardship*, 29.
245 Van Geest, *God's Earthkeepers*, 6.
246 Ibid. See Romans 1:20.
247 Ibid.
248 Ibid.
249 Ibid., 7.
250 Ibid.

PART II: IN SOCIETY

6. "God's plan of salvation includes the restoration of creation."[251] Paul writes,

> *For in him all the fullness of God was pleased to dwell, and through him to reconcile to himself all things, whether on earth or in heaven, making peace by the blood of his cross.*
>
> —Colossians 1:19–20

> *For the creation waits with eager longing for the revealing of the sons of God. For the creation was subjected to futility, not willingly, but because of him who subjected it, in hope that the creation itself will be set free from its bondage to corruption and obtain the freedom of the glory of the children of God.*
>
> —Romans 8:19–21

In short, as John Stott has said, "It would be ludicrous to suppose that God first created the earth and then handed it over to us to be destroyed."[252]

It's not about whether the science is debatable. It's about the immutable truth of Scripture.

I can imagine Paul writing the passage above from Romans 8, reflecting on how man was created to care for creation. But Paul might have thought they, first-century men and women, had come to regard all that was created before them as primarily a resource for human use, whether for industry or pleasure. The more humans simply *use* creation, the more creation attuned to the Creator awaits *"the revealing of the sons [and daughters] of God"* who will understand the responsibility of stewardship. We were designed for such stewardship, creation care, and co-curatorship, which is an earthly expression of our relationship with heaven's first citizens, the eternal Trinity.

We have a responsibility to care for creation, and particularly to care about the effect our choices have on other humans, some of whom are

---

[251] Ibid., 7.
[252] John Stott, quoted in *God's Earthkeepers* at page 9, referenced as from John Stott, "Our Human Environment," in *Decisive Issues Facing Christians Today* (Grand Rapids, MI: Fleming H. Revell, 1990), 124.

experiencing crises—displacement, illness, death—because of weather events best explained by an observed pattern of climate changes. How do we exercise our dominion responsibility?

Here are some thoughts to help you generate your own list of ideas:

- Be a Berean (Acts 17:11). Search the Scriptures for yourself. This chapter offers a foundation for you to begin that search.
- Reflect on the story of Jesus speaking to the winds and the waves (Matthew 8:23–27; Mark 4:35–41; Luke 8:22–25). Consider what it means about our relationship with God and His creation that Jesus spoke to nature, nature listened, and nature responded.
- Make time to appreciate creation and think about how nature reveals God. Every blade of grass, snowflake, flower, and leaf is similar to its own kind, and yet unique. Think about that simplicity, complexity, and design. Think about the Designer. Think about steps you can personally take to care for creation.
- Ask yourself if you have experienced or seen evidence of dramatic damage caused by seemingly uncharacteristic weather. Dig deeper. Is there evidence that human activity might have contributed to the outcome? Is there evidence it might be part of a change in historic weather patterns (a.k.a. climate change)?
- Keep the refrain, "reduce, reuse, recycle" in mind, and put it into practice. The three Rs, as this phrase is known, are intended to help us cut down on waste. And it's not just a catchy phrase. The Rs are stated in order of effect. Reduce unnecessary purchases. Consider reducing your use of non-recyclable items and packaging. Reuse items that are still useful by selling or shopping second-hand, or repurposing items you already own. Recycle in accordance with local opportunities, including giving still useable items to charity or people who you know would enjoy them.

- Participate in composting of organic materials, whether in your own yard or as part of a municipal program. Composting is often included as part of municipal recycling plans.
- Plant trees, shrubs, plants, and grass. Greenery is a net absorber of carbon dioxide and important to water absorption. I served on a municipal committee in Markham, Ontario that was charged with identifying maximum driveway sizes and minimum residential greenspace. People were paving their front lawns for parking and putting artificial surfaces in their side and backyards, resulting in a loss of water absorption during precipitation. The lack of roots and greenery resulted in excess runoff that was overwhelming the sewers and sewage treatment system in heavy rainfall, generating an environmental hazard. Greenery also plays a key role in the water cycle, recycling moisture back into the atmosphere. I learned a lot about the importance of greenery to the environment, and to municipal systems and planning.[253]

A recent Swiss study suggests that planting trees may be the most effective means of combatting climate change. Trees absorb carbon dioxide, store carbon, and have a natural cooling effect resulting from photosynthesis. All elementary school science stuff![254]

In Ethiopia, the Orthodox Tewahido Church, with nearly fifty million members, has maintained forests and greenery on property surrounding church buildings for centuries. As Ethiopia contends with consequences from decades of deforestation, the approximately thirty-five thousand church forests became oases in the desert, vital

---

[253] If your green thumb means growing something edible, that's Jeremiah 29:5-style. My dad consistently planted fruit trees along with the flowers in the yards of homes where he lived.

[254] Laura Geggel, "Want to Fight Climate Change? Plant 1 Trillion Trees," *Live Science*. July 5, 2019 (https://www.livescience.com/65880–planting-trees-fights-climate-change.html).

to the ecology of the nation.[255] The Ethiopian government recently launched a tree-planting initiative in an effort to counter the nation's deforestation.[256]

- Join or otherwise support an organization with goals that align with your heart on the issue, whether Christian (such as A Rocha) or secular (such as Ducks Unlimited).
- My friend Carl's congregation decided to bring their own cups, plates, and cutlery for church meals. When they have guests, everyone brings extra. There's no foam cups, paper plates, or plastic cutlery to dispose of; leftovers, organic waste, and dishes all leave the building after food and fellowship. Some will remember when church kitchen cupboards and drawers were filled with dinnerware and stainless steel cutlery that was washed after each use rather than plates, cups, and cutlery to be sorted into recyclables and non-recyclables for disposal after a church meal.

Be creative about caring for creation. Even though this chapter is focused on the environment, creation is more than the environment; it includes animals, fish, and more, as well as humans. Give Genesis 1 another read to fill in the blanks. Our impact on the environment affects all of creation, just as the behaviour of humans thousands of years past engendered a flood that also impacted all of creation (Genesis 6:1–9:17).

Creation points us to its Creator. Humans are part of creation. Men and women, boys and girls, have been entrusted with a special role of care for our world—partly, I think, because of our capacity to destroy it.

One aspect of citizenship responsibility for the environment is that it fits neatly into the commandments for the Church to love God, love

---

[255] Alejandro Borunda, "Ethiopia's 'Church Forests' Are Incredible Oases of Green," *National Geographic*. January 18, 2019 (https://www.nationalgeographic.com/environment/2019/01/ethiopian-church-forest-conservation-biodiversity); and Alison Abbott, "Biodiversity Thrives in Ethiopia's Church Forests," *Nature*. January 29, 2019 (https://www.nature.com/immersive/d41586-019-00275-x/index.html).

[256] Kalkidan Yibeltal, "Ethiopia 'Breaks' Tree-Planting Record to Tackle Climate Change," *BBC News*. July 29, 2019 (https://www.bbc.com/news/world-africa-49151523).

one another, and love our neighbours as we love ourselves. Another is that the responsibility to take care of creation predates all of the human institutions in which our citizenship is expressed—family, education, business, church, state, and government.

Before Church or neighbours, one man formed from the dust of the ground was given responsibility for the garden (Genesis 2:5–15). Even before a rib was removed and he became two, man and wife who are one in marriage (Genesis 2:18–25), the responsibility was given for them to co-curate. It's a vital part of our relationship one-on-one with the One who made us, a vital part of our worship.

We have developed a concept of ownership that shapes our twenty-first century thoughts about dominion. God intended that we be stewards, co-curators in partnership with Him. Stewardship informs different thinking about dominion. In Leviticus, God reminded Israel, and preserves in His Word as a reminder for us today, that we may possess the land He provides, but we cannot keep it.[257]

> *The land shall not be sold in perpetuity, for the land is mine. For you are strangers and sojourners with me.*
> —Leviticus 25:23

Paul grasped this, and wrote to the Church communicating creation's desire for us to be restored in relationship with God and return our hearts and actions to stewardship rather than ownership. It's God's wonderful creation. We get to enjoy it and care for it *with* Him.

This truth reminds me of something from my time as a chaplain to scouting troops in a church congregation Gloria and I pastored together in North Burnaby, British Columbia. The promise we said with the Beaver colony, the youngest unit in Scouting, is perhaps the biggest promise in all of the Scouting movement. It succinctly summarizes the original role given to humans: "I promise to love God and help take care of the world."

Do you?

---

[257] Gnanakan fleshes out this concept, including the responsibilities of Israel in the land, in Chapter Four of *Responsible Stewardship*, 57–70.

Three Takeaways

- Acknowledge that humans have an impact on creation, favourable or not.
- Accept that we are temporary stewards, not permanent owners, of this world.
- Commit to taking steps within our ability to leave the world better than when we arrived.

CONCLUSION

Trust in the Lord with all your heart, and do not lean on your own understanding. In all your ways acknowledge him, and he will make straight your paths. Be not wise in your own eyes; fear the Lord, and turn away from evil.

—Proverbs 3:5–7

From house to house and community to community over the last three and a half decades, we have packed and unpacked a little plaque that says "Life is fragile. Handle with prayer." It's not a quote from the Bible. It's still true. Each of us has been touched in different ways by the fragility of life. I have no idea how people who don't place their lives in the care of God get by. I've learned and continue to learn that handling life with prayer is better done in the before-moments, and still valuable in the after-moments.

Living life, including engaging our rights of citizenship in the best interest of ourselves and others, best begins with prayer.

It's easy to get distracted by our humanity, and it's easy to get distracted by our own human nature. Ken Gnanakan wrote, "Anthropocentrism places humanity at the centre. Everything in the universe is seen in terms of human utility and human interests."[258] Humans started considering where we live to be solely Man and His World long before Expo '67 used those words as its theme. That theme, and the sub-themes of Expo '67—Man the Creator, Man the Explorer, Man the Producer, Man

---

[258] Gnanakan, *Responsible Stewardship*, 84.

the Provider, and Man and the Community—were a constant message to the more than fifty million people who attended: man was at the centre of the world. And it influenced the teaching of millions more through the mandatory secondary school civics course Man in Society.

Even the Church has fallen prey to anthropocentrism, forgetting at times whose we are. Prayer reminds us who is really at the centre of life. We are reminded by Paul,

> *The God who made the world and everything in it, being Lord of heaven and earth, does not live in temples made by man, nor is he served by human hands, as though he needed anything, since he himself gives to all mankind life and breath and everything. And he made from one man every nation of mankind to live on all the face of the earth…*
> —Acts 17:24–26

He gives us life, breath, everything. God is at the centre of all life, and, when properly attuned to Him, at the centre of each life.

It's almost effortless for humans to have an even narrower perspective than anthropocentrism. Reasoning that our situation is the norm, we fall prey to self-centrism. After all, my lived experience takes place through my own eyes, ears, and emotions.

Whether we're thinking about fine points of theology, convictions in regard to human rights, or the way we are governed, our expectation can easily be that it is the same everywhere for everyone, simply because that's the way it is for me. But it's not. The rights of citizenship are different from nation to nation. Even within a nation, rights may vary between one religion and another, between men and women, or based on other state-determined or social factors. The United Nations may negotiate declarations agreed upon by the nations, but there's no consistency of recognition or application after the signatures are affixed.

Breathe. Remember who gave us breath.

Prayer reminds us that we trust in God to whom we are praying. Let's not forget the importance of the Jesus factor in changing *our* world and *the* world, the presence of Holy Spirit, and the love of our Father. Christian citizenship is exercised best when informed by the wisdom of God.

CONCLUSION

In prayer, we seek God's wisdom. In life application, we use whatever measure of the same has been entrusted to us.

Hand in glove with prayer, Christians are people of God's written Word, the Bible.

> *All Scripture is breathed out by God and profitable for teaching, for reproof, for correction, and for training in righteousness, that the man of God [and woman of God; the words used here echo the Old Testament phrase referencing a messenger of God] may be complete, equipped for every good work.*
>
> —2 Timothy 2:16–17

Although the last entry in the New Testament was made nearly two thousand years ago, and five hundred years before that in the Old Testament, there is continuing and consistent testimony that the Bible remains relevant today—not just relevant, but *as* relevant. The lessons and principles on Christian citizenship from the first century are the result of an intimate personal understanding of the Old Testament by Jesus and His first-century followers. We in turn have the benefit of their written record, the New Testament, as well as the Old Testament Scriptures they referenced, all accessibly translated into our own language.

In some countries, Christians are able to openly identify themselves, worship freely, and share their faith among themselves and with others. In other countries, being a Christian is a personal security risk. First-century Christians faced both realities while the Roman rulers were trying to gain an understanding of who they were. Were they a Jewish sect or new religion? What was the appeal of a Jewish carpenter rabbi to Greeks and Romans? Who were these people of the Way, these Christians?

Paul and others contributed to making a difference in the lives of individuals and influencing the culture of the society in which they lived. At times, these contributions were made publicly. On other occasions, privately. And always these people were messengers of God. The Gospel was shared with the most impoverished and most powerful, but the Gospel was shared, in word and in deed, in large crowds and one on one.

Like the first century, in the twenty-first century John Stackhouse reminds us,

> The most important message we have to tell, of course is the gospel of Jesus Christ. That gospel, however, is nested within the great Story of all that God has done and said, and all that God wants for us. So we have much to say, of different sorts in the public sphere today.[259]

From creation until the new heaven and new earth, we do indeed have much to say and do in the public sphere today. But foremost we are sharing the Gospel, working collaboratively with the Holy Spirit to build Jesus' Church.

One Church. One Body. Many parts.

The early Church sprang up throughout the Middle East, North Africa, Europe, and Asia as persecution pushed Christ-followers out of Jerusalem (Acts 1:8). The three most prominent expressions were Western Catholic (e.g. Roman Catholic), Eastern Orthodox (e.g. Greek Orthodox), and North African (e.g. Egyptian Coptic). In the fourth century, they came to agreement on two expressions of creed which remain the primary statements of Christian belief accepted by almost all parts of the Church: the Nicene Creed[260] (325 A.D.) and the Apostles' Creed[261] (390 A.D.).

Prayer, study of the Bible, and a creed that unifies the divided… these all inform our ability to be heaven's representatives in Earth's public sphere.

As heaven's representatives, our participation must be mindful of the old adage that we should not be so heavenly minded as to be of no earthly good. We must also not become so earthly minded as to be of no heavenly good. I have used the terms *upward-minded* and *forward-looking* to address our current opportunity to shape culture as the early Church did.

Holding dual citizenship in both heaven and earth requires balance in our pursuit of Christ's excellence. It may not always be an equal

---

[259] John G. Stackhouse, Jr., *Making the Best of It: Following Christ in the Real World* (New York, NY: Oxford University Press, 2011), 330.
[260] See Appendix I.
[261] See Appendix II.

balance. We are mindful of heaven's position on the flourishing of all things, while recognizing that our voices are not alone in the decision-making processes here on Earth. As Paul wrote, *"If possible, so far as it depends on you, live peaceably with all"* (Romans 12:18). Living peaceably with all is not the same as living privately our faith.

My experience as an openly Christian citizen in Canada has included a variety of opportunities. Fundraising for several worthy causes, Christian and not. Volunteer leadership with several charities, local and national, Christian and not. Participation in founding and leading a neighbourhood community association. Leadership of a fundraising event for our local hospital, including annual participation at the main Sunday event by the congregation instead of holding our weekly Sunday service. Sharing in the development and implementation of a motorcycle safety awareness campaign. Running municipally for political office with a campaign team of men and women from a variety of belief backgrounds.

There might not be a silver medal for finishing second in a run for public office, but this foray into politics resulted in a personal introduction that had a domino effect, leading to additional personal introductions that changed the direction of my life from pastoral ministry to public advocacy. This included public policy advocacy, lobbying of government, meeting with politicians, writing opinion editorials for national news media, taking interviews across the media spectrum, and making appearances before the Supreme Court of Canada.

At some point in my participation, not always in the beginning, it has been made known that my motivation is based on being a Christ-follower.

After three years of being the president of my neighbourhood ratepayers (taxpayers) association, another candidate decided to run against me. When asked about my motivation to do what I was doing, my answer was simple: as a Christian, this was a hands-on way to show love for my neighbours, using my skills to engage our municipal government on matters of importance to the neighbourhood.

> *...in your hearts honor Christ the Lord as holy, always being prepared to make a defense to anyone who asks you for a reason for the hope that is in you; yet do it with gentleness and respect...*
>
> —1 Peter 3:15

My experience pales in comparison to William Wilberforce, the British MP who was a leader in the move to end the slave trade, along with his friends in the Clapham Sect, a small group of reformers who planned and worked collaboratively. Wilberforce and friends gave time and money to many causes in the pursuit of re-energizing the British Church and an effort to reform the behaviour of the political leadership and population of Great Britain.

> The voluntary societies that sprang up from 1780 to 1830 numbered in the hundreds. There were groups dedicated to publishing and distributing Bibles, educating the blind, promoting animal welfare, treating ailing seamen, sponsoring vaccination efforts, and easing the plight of the poor and those in debtors' prison.
>
> Believing charity for the poor should not be confined to home, Wilberforce was also a vice president of the Friends of Foreigners in Distress.[262]

Wilberforce's book *Real Christianity* has been called the *Mere Christianity* of his day, influencing a large number of *thin* faith Christians to become *thick* faith Christians and join the reform effort.

Not one of us can do everything, but each one of us can do something. We can pray.

---

[262] Kevin Belmonte, *William Wilberforce: A Hero for Humanity* (Grand Rapids, MI: Zondervan, 2007), 160.

> God grant me the serenity to accept the things I cannot change, courage to change the things I can, and wisdom to know the difference.[263]

We all have differing measures of skill, training, education, and opportunities that enable us to also act on our prayers in pursuit of *shalom*, large scale or small. We might focus on one thing. We might space several pursuits out over a lifetime. Or like Wilberforce, we might lend ourselves and our support to many pursuits simultaneously. It takes a little wisdom to know when to get involved, how much to get involved, and when to get out. It may also take a little courage.

William Wilberforce and C.S. Lewis lived a century apart, but they shared a concern about real Christianity among Christians. Here's what Lewis wrote in *Mere Christianity*:

> And now, before I end, I am going to venture on a guess as to how this section has affected any who have read it. My guess is that there are some Leftist people among them who are very angry that it has not gone further in that direction, and some people of an opposite sort who are angry because they think it has gone much too far. If so, that brings us right up against the real snag in all the drawing up of blueprints for a Christian society. Most of us are not really approaching the subject in order to find out what Christianity says: we are approaching it in the hope of finding support from Christianity for the views of our own party. We are looking for an ally... And that is why nothing whatever is going to come of such talks unless we go a much longer way round. A Christian society is not going to arrive until most of us really want it: and we are not going to want it until we become fully Christian. I may repeat "Do as you would be done by" till I am black in the face, but I cannot

---

[263] The Serenity Prayer, written by Reinhold Niebuhr in the 1930s. See: Fred R. Shapiro, "Who Wrote the Serenity Prayer?" *The Chronicle of Higher Education*. April 28, 2014 (http://www.chronicle.com/article/Who-Wrote-the-Serenity-Prayer-/146159).

really carry it out till I love my neighbour as myself: and I cannot learn to love my neighbour as myself till I learn to love God: and I cannot learn to love God except by learning to obey Him. And so, as I warned you, we are driven on to something more inward—driven on from social matters to religious matters. For the longest way round is the shortest way home.[264]

By "a Christian society," I take Lewis to mean a society sufficiently influenced by the Church—not just identifiable buildings or institutions but the Body of all Christ-followers—to be properly adjudged Christian, although not so governed.

The question then is not so much "What would Jesus do?"[265] but, knowing the context of my life, what will I do? What will I do to *thicken* my love for God? What will I do to *thicken* my love for God's Church? What will I do to *thicken* my love for my neighbour? And what will I do to *thicken* my love for myself? And what will you do?[266]

Bob Kuhn, a Canadian lawyer and former president of Trinity Western University, has written,

> To be inspiring we must be inspired...
>
> What exactly does it mean for you to be inspired? The root meaning of "inspire" comes from the idea, "to breathe in". Simply put, we need to breathe in (be inspired) before we breathe out (be inspiring).
>
> What, or who, is the ultimate source of our inspiration. You see, "Inspiration does not come *from* us, but *through* us." This is a radical statement in today's rational, humanistic world. It takes us out of the centre of creation and compels us to recognize that we do not "own" inspiration. It is a gift. A

---

[264] Lewis, *Mere Christianity*, 78–79.
[265] This phrase was popularized in the 1990s and 2000s by a renewed interest in Charles Sheldon's 1896 novel *In His Steps: What Would Jesus Do?* (Uhrichsville, OH: Barbour and Company, Inc., 1993).
[266] John Stackhouse suggests the question to be asked is: "What would Jesus want me, or us, to do here and now?" (Stackhouse, *Why You're Here*, 75).

gift we must share in our own unique way... We cannot keep it to ourselves. We must breathe out.[267]

Breathe in. Then breathe out.

To engage our world as ambassadors for Christ (2 Corinthians 5:20), we must first be devoted citizens of heaven. Breathing heaven in, and breathing heaven out, on Earth.

Canadian author and Bible dramatist David Kitz has stated succinctly,

> Make no mistake; Jesus calls us to be citizens in his heavenly Kingdom. It is a Kingdom that is headquartered in heaven, but its address on the earth is the human heart—your heart—my heart.[268]

It is from our earthly address that we engage with people, creation, and the world around us, mindful that we are always sowing seeds. We do not know where, when, or how the seeds will sprout, grow, and hopefully bear fruit. Let them be good seeds.

Even with encouraging words framed by Kuhn and Kitz, it can be scary to think of engaging publicly with a *Jesus* tag affixed to our person for all to see.

Another Canadian, Christine MacMillan, has some helpful words of advice. In life, MacMillan started shy and is finishing strong. A social worker who became a Salvation Army officer, MacMillan retired after having been the national leader in Canada and the founding director of the Salvation Army International Social Justice Committee, based in New York to be near the United Nations. Within months of retirement she took on responsibilities with the World Evangelical Alliance, retiring in 2018 from the position of Associate Secretary General for Public Engagement. MacMillan continues to work with the WEA's Global Human

---

267 Bob Kuhn, "You Inspire Me," *Positively Parkinson's*. May 18, 2019 (http://positivelyparkinsons.blogspot.com/2019/05/you-inspire-me.html).
268 David Kitz, "Our Conquering Hero," *I Love the Psalms*. May 8, 2019 (https://davidkitz.blog/2019/05/08/our-conquering-hero).

Trafficking Task Force and the United Nations. Here are her words of advice about moving from inspiration to application:

> Will you make a big impact on others? Absolutely. But remember to give God the glory and thanksgiving for the transformation that is brought about through your ministry. God is *your* leader. Follow His lead. Be willing to step out of your comfort zone, to be stretched, to be moulded. Be willing to learn and have a teachable spirit so that God can train you to meet every challenge.[269]

The others you influence may be few or many, but you will make a big impact when you follow His lead.

The twenty-first-century version of the first-century Church council that accepted Gentiles into the Church (Acts 15:6–29) and the early Church councils that gave us the creeds might well be the conversations that take place between the World Evangelical Alliance, World Council of Churches, and the Pontifical Council for Interreligious Dialogue (the Vatican). These three have member organizations and affiliates that represent almost every Christian on Earth. In 2011, they released a short but important document entitled *Christian Witness in a Multi-Religious World: Recommendations for Conduct*.[270] In list form, here are ten principles they agreed upon.

1. Act in God's love.
2. Imitate Jesus Christ.
3. Demonstrate Christian virtues.
4. Perform acts of service and justice.
5. Use discernment and wisdom.
6. Reject violence.
7. Endorse freedom of religion and belief.
8. Mutual respect.

---

[269] Lang, *Faith, Life and Leadership*, 94. MacMillan also tells her career story in the chapter entitled "Pursuing a World View of Poverty and Social Justice."
[270] See Appendix III.

9. Renounce false witness.
10. Build relationship.

Those are principles for good seeds and good sowing. You can read the brief detail for each of these points in Appendix III.

In the Preface, I stated my desire to both inform and challenge your perspective on citizenship as a Christian. I hope that has been accomplished.

In the course of this book, however, I have left out one important message about our engagement in the world as dual citizens. It's a warning from Jesus about the reality of opening the doors of our prayer closets and worship spaces to go out into the society in which we live:

> *Behold, I am sending you out as sheep in the midst of wolves, so be wise as serpents and innocent as doves.*
>
> —Matthew 10:16

Jesus continued in the same discourse to advise that we should expect poor treatment, even abusive treatment, from those who disagree with us. They disagree with Him.[271] That was the experience of Christ-followers in the first century and is the experience of more than 245 million Christians globally today. The other two billion of us ought not to be surprised when poor treatment is directed our way.

Preston Manning, the Canadian politician and author who founded a political party in western Canada that became a nationwide movement and eventually merged with (some say consumed) the national conservative political party, commented on Jesus' words thusly:

> Jesus said, "Behold, I send you forth as sheep in the midst of wolves: be ye therefore wise as serpents, and harmless as doves," (Matthew 10:16, KJV) not vicious as snakes and stupid as pigeons.[272]

---

271 Matthew 10 is a sobering and encouraging chapter to read.
272 Preston Manning, "Lessons from the Life and Teachings of Jesus," Navigating the Faith-Political Interface (seminar). Toronto, Ontario. May 11, 2007.

CHURCH IN SOCIETY

By that, Manning humorously reminds us that the world is unfriendly, but if it is unfriendly toward us because of our behaviour rather than for Christ's name's sake, then that is our fault, having more to do with us than Him. Let us neither be vicious nor foolish in our representation of Christ or our treatment of others. If we ourselves are to be treated poorly, let it be because we are living well for Jesus.

Of course, citizenship is about more than politics. And Christian citizenship is about even more. Disciples of Jesus were first called Christians at Antioch (Acts 11:26), but this was not a name they chose for themselves. Essentially meaning "You little anointed ones, followers of the One you call Christ," it was not a complimentary term. Neither was it the name used by Christ-followers to refer to themselves. They called one another *saints*, a word Paul used more than three dozen times in nine of his letters, and John more than a dozen times in the Book of Revelation. *Saint* meant sacred, sanctified, consecrated to God... set apart for God.[273] It didn't mean they were set apart from other parts of the Church, or set apart *from* the world. It meant they were set apart for God's purposes *in* the world.

The final word, an inspired word that captures the thrust of this book, belongs to Paul, our citizen model from the first century. Paul was born into Roman citizenship and had to be born again to acquire citizenship in heaven (John 3:3). Paul lived, taught, and wrote about the life of dual citizenship. He provided for us the following succinct words of advice, which are a first-century reverberation of the words of Micah 6:8 found as the epigraph at the front of this book.

As we move to Paul's closing words, don't just do so in order to set this book aside. Let your life similarly bear witness to a twenty-first-century resonance of Micah 6:8, faithfulness to Christ, and to the first-century testimony of Paul and his compatriots. Entrust your life to Christ to be an integral part of the Church in society, upward-minded and forward-thinking as you engage the world as a citizen-ambassador of heaven and citizen on Earth.

---

[273] Definition derived from James Strong, *Strong's Exhaustive Concordance, Greek Dictionary of the New Testament*, #40.

CONCLUSION

For the guidance of saints on the Way, for *our* guidance, Paul asserts simply and profoundly, *"If we live by the Spirit, let us also keep in step with the Spirit"* (Galatians 5:25).

Three Takeaways

- Love the Lord our God with all your heart and soul and mind and strength.
- Love one another, and by this the world will know we are His disciples.
- Love your neighbour as yourself.

EPILOGUE, THE DUAL CITIZENS' PRAYER

Our Father in heaven, hallowed be your name. Your kingdom come, your will be done, on earth as it is in heaven. Give us this day our daily bread, and forgive us our debts, as we also have forgiven our debtors. And lead us not into temptation, but deliver us from evil. [Some manuscripts add, "For yours is the kingdom and the power and the glory, forever. Amen."]

—Matthew 6:9–13

Three Takeaways

- The message of a first-century prayer is a reminder that Christ, not man (or woman), is the hope of the world.
- Christians who desire and participate in His will being done on Earth give hope to society.
- Influencing tomorrow requires that today we love and trust the Lord our God with all.

APPENDIX I: THE NICENE CREED

325 A.D., Council of Nicaea
Amended in 381 A.D., Council of Constantinople

We believe in one God, the Father, the Almighty, maker of heaven and earth, of all that is seen and unseen. We believe in one Lord, Jesus Christ, the only Son of God, eternally begotten of the Father, God from God, light from light, true God from true God, begotten, not made, one in Being with the Father. For us and for our salvation he came down from heaven, by the power of the Holy Spirit he was born of the Virgin Mary and became truly human. For our sake he was crucified under Pontius Pilate; he suffered, died and was buried. On the third day he rose again in fulfillment of the Scriptures; he ascended into heaven and is seated at the right hand of the Father. He will come again in glory to judge the living and the dead, and his kingdom will have no end. We believe in the Holy Spirit, the Lord, the giver of life, who proceeds from the Father [and the Son]. Who with the Father and the Son is worshiped and glorified. Who has spoken through the prophets. We believe in one holy catholic and apostolic Church. We acknowledge one baptism for the forgiveness of sins. We look for the resurrection of the dead, and the life of the world to come. Amen.

APPENDIX II: THE APOSTLES' CREED

390 A.D.

Recorded in a letter from Ambrose, Bishop of Milan, to Pope Siricius, Bishop of Rome, following the Council in Milan

> I believe in God, the Father, the Almighty,
> Creator of heaven and earth,
> I believe in Jesus Christ, His only Son, our Lord,
> Who was conceived by the Holy Ghost, born of the Virgin Mary,
> He suffered under Pontius Pilate, was crucified, died, and was buried,
> He descended into hell; the third day He rose again from the dead,
> He ascended into heaven, is seated at the right hand of God the Father Almighty; thence He
> shall come to judge the living and the dead.
> I believe in the Holy Spirit, the holy catholic Church, the communion of saints, forgiveness of
> sins, the resurrection of the body and the life everlasting.
> Amen.

APPENDIX III

Christian Witness in a Multi-Religious World: Recommendations for Conduct as issued by World Council of Churches, Pontifical Council for Interreligious Dialogue and World Evangelical Alliance (2011).

Preamble

Mission belongs to the very being of the church. Proclaiming the word of God and witnessing to the world is essential for every Christian. At the same time, it is necessary to do so according to gospel principles, with full respect and love for all human beings.

Aware of the tensions between people and communities of different religious convictions and the varied interpretations of Christian witness, the Pontifical Council for Interreligious Dialogue (PCID), the World Council of Churches (WCC) and, at the invitation of the WCC, the World Evangelical Alliance (WEA), met during a period of 5 years to reflect and produce this document to serve as a set of recommendations for conduct on Christian witness around the world. This document does not intend to be a theological statement on mission but to address practical issues associated with Christian witness in a multi-religious world.

The purpose of this document is to encourage churches, church councils and mission agencies to reflect on their current practices and to use the recommendations in this document to prepare, where appropriate, their own guidelines for their witness and mission among those of different religions and among those who do not profess any particular religion. It is hoped that Christians across the world will study this document in the light of their own practices in witnessing to their faith in Christ, both by word and deed.

A basis for Christian witness

1. For Christians it is a privilege and joy to give an accounting for the hope that is within them and to do so with gentleness and respect (cf. 1 Peter 3:15).

2. Jesus Christ is the supreme witness (cf. John 18:37). Christian witness is always a sharing in his witness, which takes the form of proclamation of the kingdom, service to neighbour and the total gift of self even if that act of giving leads to the cross. Just as the Father sent the Son in the power of the Holy Spirit, so believers are sent in mission to witness in word and action to the love of the triune God.

3. The example and teaching of Jesus Christ and of the early church must be the guides for Christian mission. For two millennia Christians have sought to follow Christ's way by sharing the good news of God's kingdom (cf. Luke 4:16–20).

4. Christian witness in a pluralistic world includes engaging in dialogue with people of different religions and cultures (cf. Acts 17:22–28).

5. In some contexts, living and proclaiming the gospel is difficult, hindered or even prohibited, yet Christians are commissioned by Christ to continue faithfully in solidarity with one another in their witness to him (cf. Matthew 28:19–20; Mark 16:14–18; Luke 24:44–48; John 20:21; Acts 1:8).

6. If Christians engage in inappropriate methods of exercising mission by resorting to deception and coercive means, they betray the gospel and may cause suffering to others. Such

departures call for repentance and remind us of our need for God's continuing grace (cf. Romans 3:23).

7. Christians affirm that while it is their responsibility to witness to Christ, conversion is ultimately the work of the Holy Spirit (cf. John 16:7–9; Acts 10:44–47). They recognize that the Spirit blows where the Spirit wills in ways over which no human being has control (cf. John 3:8).

Principles

Christians are called to adhere to the following principles as they seek to fulfil Christ's commission in an appropriate manner, particularly within interreligious contexts.

1. *Acting in God's love.* Christians believe that God is the source of all love and, accordingly, in their witness they are called to live lives of love and to love their neighbour as themselves (cf. Matthew 22:34–40; John 14:15).

2. *Imitating Jesus Christ.* In all aspects of life, and especially in their witness,

Christians are called to follow the example and teachings of Jesus Christ, sharing his love, giving glory and honour to God the Father in the power of the Holy Spirit (cf. John 20:21–23).

3. *Christian virtues.* Christians are called to conduct themselves with integrity, charity, compassion and humility, and to overcome all arrogance, condescension and disparagement (cf. Galatians 5:22).

4. *Acts of service and justice.* Christians are called to act justly and to love tenderly (cf. Micah 6:8). They are further called to serve others and in so doing to recognize Christ in the least of their sisters and brothers (cf. Matthew 25:45). Acts of service, such as providing education, health care, relief services and acts of justice and advocacy are an integral part of witnessing to the gospel. The exploitation of situations of poverty and need has no place in Christian outreach. Christians should denounce and

refrain from offering all forms of allurements, including financial incentives and rewards, in their acts of service.

5. *Discernment in ministries of healing.* As an integral part of their witness to the gospel, Christians exercise ministries of healing. They are called to exercise discernment as they carry out these ministries, fully respecting human dignity and ensuring that the vulnerability of people and their need for healing are not exploited.

6. *Rejection of violence.* Christians are called to reject all forms of violence, even psychological or social, including the abuse of power in their witness. They also reject violence, unjust discrimination or repression by any religious or secular authority, including the violation or destruction of places of worship, sacred symbols or texts.

7. *Freedom of religion and belief.* Religious freedom including the right to publicly profess, practice, propagate and change one's religion flows from the very dignity of the human person which is grounded in the creation of all human beings in the image and likeness of God (cf. Genesis 1:26). Thus, all human beings have equal rights and responsibilities. Where any religion is instrumentalized for political ends, or where religious persecution occurs, Christians are called to engage in a prophetic witness denouncing such actions.

8. *Mutual respect and solidarity.* Christians are called to commit themselves to work with all people in mutual respect, promoting together justice, peace and the common good. Interreligious cooperation is an essential dimension of such commitment.

9. *Respect for all people.* Christians recognize that the gospel both challenges and enriches cultures. Even when the gospel challenges certain aspects of cultures, Christians are called to respect all people. Christians are also called to discern elements in their own cultures that are challenged by the gospel.

10. *Renouncing false witness.* Christians are to speak sincerely and respectfully; they are to listen in order to learn

about and understand others' beliefs and practices, and are encouraged to acknowledge and appreciate what is true and good in them. Any comment or critical approach should be made in a spirit of mutual respect, making sure not to bear false witness concerning other religions.

11. *Ensuring personal discernment.* Christians are to acknowledge that changing one's religion is a decisive step that must be accompanied by sufficient time for adequate reflection and preparation, through a process ensuring full personal freedom.

12. *Building interreligious relationships.* Christians should continue to build relationships of respect and trust with people of different religions so as to facilitate deeper mutual understanding, reconciliation and cooperation for the common good.

Recommendations

The Third Consultation organized by the World Council of Churches and the PCID of the Holy See in collaboration with World Evangelical Alliance with participation from the largest Christian families of faith (Catholic, Orthodox, Protestant, Evangelical and Pentecostal), having acted in a spirit of ecumenical cooperation to prepare this document for consideration by churches, national and regional confessional bodies and mission organizations, and especially those working in interreligious contexts, recommends that these bodies:

1. *study* the issues set out in this document and where appropriate formulate guidelines for conduct regarding Christian witness applicable to their particular contexts. Where possible this should be done ecumenically, and in consultation with representatives of other religions.

2. *build* relationships of respect and trust with people of all religions, in particular at institutional levels between churches and other religious communities, engaging in on-going interreligious dialogue as part of their Christian commitment. In

certain contexts, where years of tension and conflict have created deep suspicions and breaches of trust between and among communities, interreligious dialogue can provide new opportunities for resolving conflicts, restoring justice, healing of memories, reconciliation and peace-building.

3. *encourage* Christians to strengthen their own religious identity and faith while deepening their knowledge and understanding of different religions, and to do so also taking into account the perspectives of the adherents of those religions. Christians should avoid misrepresenting the beliefs and practices of people of different religions.

4. *cooperate* with other religious communities engaging in interreligious advocacy towards justice and the common good and, wherever possible, standing together in solidarity with people who are in situations of conflict.

5. *call* on their governments to ensure that freedom of religion is properly and comprehensively respected, recognizing that in many countries religious institutions and persons are inhibited from exercising their mission.

6. *pray* for their neighbours and their well-being, recognizing that prayer is integral to who we are and what we do, as well as to Christ's mission.

Appendix: Background to the document

1. In today's world there is increasing collaboration among Christians and between Christians and followers of different religions. The Pontifical Council for Interreligious Dialogue (PCID) of the Holy See and the World Council of Churches' Programme on Interreligious Dialogue and Co-operation (WCC-IRDC) have a history of such collaboration. Examples of themes on which the PCID/WCC-IRDC have collaborated in the past are: Interreligious Marriage (1994–1997), Interreligious Prayer (1997–1998) and African Religiosity (2000–2004). This document is a result of their work together.

2. There are increasing interreligious tensions in the world today, including violence and the loss of human life. Politics, economics and other factors play a role in these tensions. Christians too are sometimes involved in these conflicts, whether voluntarily or involuntarily, either as those who are persecuted or as those participating in violence. In response to this the PCID and WCC-IRDC decided to address the issues involved in a joint process towards producing shared recommendations for conduct on Christian witness. The WCC-IRDC invited the World Evangelical Alliance (WEA) to participate in this process, and they have gladly done so.

3. Initially two consultations were held: the first, in Lariano, Italy, in May 2006, was entitled "Assessing the Reality" where representatives of different religions shared their views and experiences on the question of conversion. A statement from the consultation reads in part: "We affirm that, while everyone has a right to invite others to an understanding of their faith, it should not be exercised by violating others' rights and religious sensibilities. Freedom of religion enjoins upon all of us the equally non-negotiable responsibility to respect faiths other than our own, and never to denigrate, vilify or misrepresent them for the purpose of affirming superiority of our faith."

4. The second, an inter-Christian consultation, was held in Toulouse, France, in August 2007, to reflect on these same issues. Questions on Family and Community, Respect for Others, Economy, Marketing and Competition, and Violence and Politics were thoroughly discussed. The pastoral and missionary issues around these topics became the background for theological reflection and for the principles developed in this document. Each issue is important in its own right and deserves more attention that can be given in these recommendations.

5. The participants of the third (inter-Christian) consultation met in Bangkok, Thailand, from 25–28, January, 2011 and finalized this document.

BIBLIOGRAPHY

Bibles

Dennis, Lane T. and Wayne Grudem, eds. *The ESV Study Bible* (Wheaton, IL: Crossway, 2011).

ESV® Bible (The Holy Bible, English Standard Version®), copyright © 2001 by Crossway, a publishing ministry of Good News Publishers (Wheaton, IL: Crossway, 2007).

Harper, Albert F., ed. *The Wesley Bible: A Personal Study Bible for Holy Living* (Nashville, TN: Thomas Nelson Publishers, 1990).

The Holy Bible, New King James Version, copyright © 1982 by Thomas Nelson, Inc.

Holy Bible, King James Version, public domain.

New American Standard Bible: The Open Bible Edition (Nashville, TN: Thomas Nelson, Publishers, 1979).

New American Standard Bible, copyright ©1977 by The Lockman Foundation.

Stamps, Donald C., ed. *Fire Bible: English Standard Version* (Peabody, MA: Hendrickson Publishers Marketing LLC, 2014).

The Holy Bible: The Amplified Bible (La Habra, CA: The Lockman Foundation, 1987).

Thompson, Frank Charles, ed. *The Thompson Chain Reference Bible: New International Version* (Indianapolis, IN: B.B. Kirkbride Bible Co., Inc., 1983).

YouVersion Bible App (Edmund, OK: Life.Church, https://www.youversion.com/, accessed May 30, 2019).

Published Sources

Abbott, Alison. "Biodiversity Thrives in Ethiopia's Church Forests," *Nature*. January 29, 2019 (https://www.nature.com/immersive/d41586-019-00275-x/index.html).

Amity Foundation, The. *The Amity Foundation: 30th Anniversary, Footprints of Love* (Nanjing, JS: The Amity Foundation, 2015).

Belmonte, Kevin. *William Wilberforce: A Hero for Humanity* (Grand Rapids, MI: Zondervan, 2007).

Berton, Pierre. *The Comfortable Pew: A Critical Look at the Church in the New Age* (Toronto, ON: McLelland and Stewart, 1965).

Bonhoeffer, Dietrich. *The Cost of Discipleship* (London, UK: SCM Press Ltd., 1949).

Borg, Marcus J. *Evolution of the Word: The New Testament in the Order the Books Were Written* (New York, NY: HarperCollins Publishers, 2012).

Borunda, Alejandro. "Ethiopia's 'Church Forests' Are Incredible Oases of Green," *National Geographic*. January 18, 2019 (https://www.nationalgeographic.com/environment/2019/01/ethiopian-church-forest-conservation-biodiversity)

"Brief History of L'Arche, A" *L'Arche Canada*. Date of access: May 13, 2019 (https://www.larche.ca/about-larche/our-history).

Bruce, F.F. *Paul: Apostle of the Heart Set Free* (Grand Rapids, MI: Chosen Books, 1991).

---. *The New Testament Documents: Are They Reliable?* (Grand Rapids, MI: Eerdmans, 1960).

Campolo, Tony, and Mary Albert Darling. *Connecting Like Jesus: Practices for Healing, Teaching, and Preaching* (San Francisco, CA: Jossey-Bass, 2010).

"Canada Summer Jobs Court Cases," appeal letter, *The Evangelical Fellowship of Canada*. March 7, 2019 (https://www.evangelicalfellowship.ca/Get-involved/Support-the-EFC/Appeal-letters/2019/Canada-Summer-Jobs-Court-Cases).

Canadian Bible Society. *The Bible Explored 2: A Short History* (Canada: Canadian Bible Society, 2015).

Casper, Jayson. "Sri Lankan Sunday School Was 'Willing to Die for Christ' on Easter. Half Did," *Christianity Today*. April 25, 2019 (https://www.christianitytoday.com/news/2019/april/sri-lanka-easter-isis-zion-Sunday-school-sebastian-funerals.html).

Chambers, Oswald. *My Utmost for His Highest: Selections for the Year* (New York, NY: Dodd, Mead & Company, 1935).

"Changing Global Religious Landscape, The" *Pew Research Centre*. April 5, 2017 (http://www.pewforum.org/2017/04/05/the-changing-global-religious-landscape).

Chaplin, Jonathan. "The Point of Kuyperian Pluralism," *Comment Magazine*. November 1, 2013 (https://www.cardus.ca/comment/article/4069/the-point-of-kuyperian-pluralism).

Character Community, York Region. Date of access: May 17, 2019 (https://www.charactercommunity.com).

Chevrau, Guy. *Catch the Fire: The Toronto Blessing, An Experience of Renewal and Revival* (Toronto, ON: HarperPerennial, 1995).

Christian Witness in a Multi-Religious World: Recommendations for Conduct, World Council of Churches, Pontifical Council for Interreligious Dialogue, World Evangelical Alliance, June 28, 2011.

"Church Attendance," *Outreach Canada*, June 27, 2016 (https://www.outreach.ca/resources/research/ArticleId/613/Church-Attendance).

Davy, Alston E. *Saul of Tarsus, A Compendium: Sinner, Saint, Apostate or Apostle?* (Markham, ON: Alpha Communications, 2017).

De Souza, Raymond J., Mark Carney, and Roger Martin. "God, Greed & Gaming," *Convivium Magazine*. June 7, 2013 (https://www.convivium.ca/articles/god-greed-gaming).

Fahmy, Dalia. "European Countries that Have Mandatory Church Taxes Are About as Religious as Their Neighbors that Don't," *Pew Research Centre*. May 9, 2019 (https://www.pewresearch.org/fact-tank/2019/05/09/european-countries-that-have-mandatory-church-taxes-are-about-as-religious-as-their-neighbors-that-dont).

Foxe, John and Voice of the Martyrs. *Foxe: Voices of the Martyrs—33 A.D to Today* (Orlando, FL: Bridge-Logos, 2007).

Fletcher, Cliff. "Freedom, Government and Appropriate Response: Canada Summer Jobs," *The Free Methodist Church in Canada*. January 2, 2018 (https://www.fmcic.ca/cliffsnotes-january-2-2018).

Frisse, Ulrich. *Building Communities of Belonging: The Ongoing Story of Christian Horizons* (Kitchener, ON: Historical Branding Solutions, Inc., 2016).

Geddes, John. "Liberals Move to Defuse Canada Summer Jobs Controversy," *Maclean's*. December 6, 2018 (https://www.macleans.ca/politics/ottawa/liberals-move-to-defuse-canada-summer-jobs-controversy).

Geggel, Laura. "Want to Fight Climate Change? Plant 1 Trillion Trees," *Live Science*. July 5, 2019 (https://www.livescience.com/65880-planting-trees-fights-climate-change.html).

Gnanakan, Ken, World Evangelical Alliance Theological Commission. *Responsible Stewardship of God's Creation* (Bangalore, KA: Theological Book Trust, 2004).

Gottheil, Richard and Wilhelm Bacher. "Aramaic Language Among the Jews," *Jewish Encyclopedia* (http://www.jewishencyclopedia.com/articles/1707–aramaic-language-among-the-jews).

Grant, George. *Lament for a Nation: The Defeat of Canadian Nationalism, 40th Anniversary Edition* (Montreal, QC: McGill-Queen's University Press, 2005).

Greene, Mark and Catherine Butcher. *The Servant Queen and the King She Serves, with a foreword by Her Majesty Queen Elizabeth II* (London, UK: Bible Society, HOPE, LICC, 2016).

Haskell, David M. *Through a Lens Darkly: How the News Media Perceive and Portray Evangelicals* (Toronto, ON: Clements Academic, 2009).

Hayhoe, Katharine. "6 Myths About Climate Change Debunked," *Châtelaine*. April 10, 2019 (https://www.chatelaine.com/living/climate-change-myths-debunked-by-scientist).

Hill, Barbara. *Historic Churches of Barbados* (Bridgetown, BB: Art Heritage Publications, 1984).

"How It All Began," *Christian Horizons*. Date of access: May 13, 2019 (https://www.christian-horizons.org/who-we-are/history).

Hug, Adam, ed. *Traditional Religion and Political Power: Examining the Role of the Church in Georgia, Armenia, Ukraine and Moldova* (London, UK: The Foreign Policy Centre, 2015).

Hulme, Mike. "Climate Change (Concept of)," *The International Encyclopedia of Geography*. Date of access: May 30, 2019 (https://www.academia.edu/10358797/Climate_change_concept_of).

Hurtado, Larry W. *Destroyer of the gods: Early Christian Distinctiveness in the Roman World* (Waco, TX: Baylor University Press, 2016).

Hutchinson, Don. *Under Siege: Religious Freedom and the Church in Canada at 150 (1867–2017)* (Winnipeg, MB: Word Alive Press, 2017).

International Commission of Jurists. *A Primer on International Human Rights Law and Standards on the Right to Freedom of Thought, Conscience, Religion or Belief* (Geneva, Switzerland: International Commission of Jurists, 2019).

Johnston, Jeremiah J. *Unimaginable: What Our World Would Be Like Without Christianity* (Minneapolis, MN: Bethany House Publishers, 2017).

Josephus, Flavius. *The Genuine Works of Flavius Josephus the Jewish Historian*, William Whiston, trans., *The Antiquities of the Jews* and *The Jewish War; or, The History of the Destruction of Jerusalem* (http://penelope.uchicago.edu/josephus/index.html).

Kitz, David. "Our Conquering Hero," *I Love the Psalms*. May 8, 2019 (https://davidkitz.blog/2019/05/08/our-conquering-hero).

Kuchma, Anna. "Where Does the Russian Orthodox Church Get Its Money From?" *Russia Beyond*. March 9, 2016 (https://www.rbth.com/business/2016/03/09/where-does-the-russian-orthodox-church-get-its-money-from_574079).

Kuhn, Bob. "You Inspire Me," *Positively Parkinson's*. May 18, 2019 (http://positivelyparkinsons.blogspot.com/2019/05/you-inspire-me.html).

Ladd, George Eldon. *The Gospel of the Kingdom: Scriptural Studies in the Kingdom of God* (Grand Rapids, MI: Wm. B. Eerdmans Publishing Co, 2002). First published in 1959.

Lang, Georgialee, ed. *Faith, Life and Leadership: 8 Canadian Women Tell Their Stories* (Belleville, ON: Castle Quay Books, 2017).

Langford, Thomas A. *Practical Divinity: Theology for the Wesleyan Tradition* (Nashville, TN: Abingdon Press, 1983).

"Launch of the Chinese Study Bible," *United Bible Societies China Partnership*. January 17, 2018 (https://www.ubscp.org/launch-chinese-studybible).

Lewis, Clive Staples (C.S.). *Mere Christianity* (London, UK: Fontana Books, 1952).

---. *The Four Loves* (Glasgow, UK: William Collins and Co Ltd, 1979).

Manning, Preston. "Lessons from the Life and Teachings of Jesus," Navigating the Faith-Political Interface (seminar). Toronto, Ontario. May 11, 2007.

Marsh, J.H., ed. *The Canadian Encyclopedia, Second Edition* (Edmonton, AB: Hurtig Publishers, 1988).

McCluskey, Megan. "Queen Elizabeth Is Turning 92 Years Old. Here's Why She Has Two Birthdays," *TIME*. April 20, 2018 (http://time.com/5248082/queen-elizabeth-two-birthdays).

McLoughlin, Barry J., "Encountering the Media: A Seminar by McLoughlin Media," Ottawa, Canada. August 27–29, 2008.

---. *Encountering the Media: Media Strategies and Techniques* (Ottawa, ON: McLoughlin Multi-Media Strategies, 2005).

Mears, Henrietta. *What the Bible Is All About* (Ventura, CA: Regal Books, 1985). First edition published in 1953.

Mother Teresa of Calcutta. *A Gift for God* (London, UK: Collins, 1975).

Muggeridge, Malcolm. *Christ and the Media* (Grand Rapids, MI: William B. Eerdmans Publishing Company, 1977).

Neutel, Jennifer. "Q&A with Lorna Dueck," *Christian Courier*. April 11, 2016 (http://www.christiancourier.ca/news/entry/qa-with-lorna-dueck).

Nouwen, Henri. *In the Name of Jesus: Reflections on Christian Leadership* (New York, NY: The Crossroad Publishing Company, 1989).

Open Doors International. Date of access: April 20, 2019 (www.opendoors.org).

Open Doors. *2019 World Watch List: A Guide to Global Persecution* (Halton Hills, ON: Open Doors Canada, 2019).

Packer, J.I., *Knowing God* (Downers Grove, IL: Intervarsity Press, 1973).

Pollock, John. *The Apostle: A Life of Paul* (Colorado Springs, CO: David C. Cook, 2011).

Prizant, Barry M., with Tom Fields-Meyer. *Uniquely Human: A Different Way of Seeing Autism* (New York, NY: Simon & Schuster Paperbacks, 2015).

Redekop, John H. "Christians and Civil Disobedience: A Background Paper by the Religious Liberty Commission of The Evangelical Fellowship of Canada." Revised August 2001.

---. *Politics Under God* (Waterloo, ON: Herald Press, 2007).

Rees, Matthew. *2019 World Watch List Report: The Rise of Religious Persecution Across the World* (Halton Hills, ON: Open Doors Canada, 2019).

Revell Bible Dictionary, The (Grand Rapids, MI: Fleming H. Revell, 1990).

Rinehart, John. *Gospel Patrons: People Whose Generosity Changed the World* (Minneapolis, MN: Reclaimed Publishing, 2016).

Robinson, Benjamin W. "An Ephesian Imprisonment of Paul," *Journal of Biblical Literature*, Volume 29, Number 2 (1910): 181–89 (http://www.jstor.org/stable/4617113)

Rowe, Lynette. "He Didn't Say that It Would Be Easy" (song lyrics), 1981.

Salvation Army, The. *The Salvation Army Handbook of Doctrine* (London, UK: Salvation Books, 2010). Access the PDF edition at: https://s3.amazonaws.com/cache.salvationarmy.org/26defc89-e794-4e5a-a567-0793f3742430_English+Handbook+of+Doctrine+web.pdf

Samaan, Magdy and Declan Walsh. "Egypt Declares State of Emergency, as Attacks Undercut Promise of Security," *New York Times*. April 9, 2017 (https://www.nytimes.com/2017/04/09/world/middleeast/explosion-egypt-coptic-christian-church.html).

Schottelkorb, Kerry, and Joann Pittman. "China Tells Christianity To Be More Chinese," *Christianity Today*. March 20, 2019 (https://www.christianitytoday.com/news/2019/march/sinicization-china-wants-christianity-churches-more-chinese.html).

"Scripture Impact Since 1985," *United Bible Societies China Partnership*. Date of access: January 2, 2018 (https://www.ubscp.org/scripture-impact).

Shapiro, Fred R. "Who Wrote the Serenity Prayer?" *The Chronicle of Higher Education*. April 28, 2014 (http://www.chronicle.com/article/Who-Wrote-the-Serenity-Prayer-/146159).

Sheldon, Charles. *In His Steps: What Would Jesus Do?* (Uhrichsville, OH: Barbour and Company, Inc., 1993). Originally published in 1896.

Smith, Dean. "Egyptian Cave Church Has 70,000 People Attending Services Every Week," *Open the Word*. July 5, 2016 (https://opentheword.org/2016/07/05/egyptian-cave-church-has-70000-people-attending-services-every-week).

Sputo, Dominic, with Brian Smith. *Heirloom Love: Authentic Christianity for This Age of Persecution* (Canada: Dominic Sputo, 2016).

Stackhouse, John G., Jr. *Making the Best of It: Following Christ in the Real World* (New York, NY: Oxford University Press, 2011).

---. *Why You're Here: Ethics for the Real World* (New York, NY: Oxford University Press, 2018).

"Status of Global Christianity, 2019, in the Context of 1900–2050," *Gordon Conwell Theological Seminary*. Date of access: September 19, 2019 (https://gordonconwell.edu/wp-content/uploads/sites/13/2019/04/StatusofGlobalChristianity20191.pdf).

Strobel, Lee. *The Case for Christmas: A Journalist Investigates the Identity of the Child in the Manger* (Grand Rapids, MI: Zondervan, 2005).

Strong, James. *Strong's Exhaustive Concordance* (Grand Rapids, MI: Baker Book House, 1980).

Swindoll, Charles R. *Hand Me Another Brick: Timeless Lessons on Leadership—How Effective Leaders Motivate Themselves and Others* (Nashville, TN: Thomas Nelson, 2006).

---., *Paul: A Man of Grace and Grit: Profiles in Character* (Nashville, TN: Thomas Nelson, 2002).

---. "Tools," *Insight for Living Ministries*. April 26, 2015 (https://www.insight.org/resources/daily-devotional/individual/tools).

Toycen, Dave. *The Power of Generosity: How to Transform Yourself and Your World* (Toronto, ON: HarperCollins Publishers Ltd., 2004).

Tuttle, George M. *The Christian as Citizen* (Canada: Publications Committee, Department of Education, Canadian Council of Churches, 1949).

"Two-Thirds of Population Declare Christian as Their Religion," *Statistics Canada*. February 19, 2016 (https://www150.statcan.gc.ca/n1/pub/91-003-x/2014001/section03/33-eng.htm).

United Nations

---. *Charter of the United Nations*, 26 June 1945, Can TS 1945.

---. *International Covenant on Civil and Political Rights*, 19 December 1966, 999 UNTS 171, Can TS 1976 No. 47 (entered into force 23 March 1976).

---. *United Nations Declaration on the Elimination of All Forms of Intolerance and of Discrimination based on Religion or Belief*, GA Res.36/55, UN GAOR Supp. (no. 51) 71, UN Doc. A/36/51 (1981).

---. *Universal Declaration of Human Rights*, 10 December 1948, GA Res.217 A (III), UN GAOR, 3rd sess., Supp. No. 13, UN Doc. A/810 (1948) 71.

---. *Paris Agreement to the United Nations Framework Convention on Climate Change*, Dec. 12, 2015, T.I.A.S. No. 16–1104 (entered into force 4 November 2016).

---. "Report of the International Law Commission to the General Assembly, Part II. Ways and Means of Making the Evidence of Customary International Law More Readily Available," *Yearbook of the International Law Commission*, [1950] 2 Y.B. Int'l L. Comm'n 367, U.N. Doc. A/CN.4/Ser.A/1950/Add.1 (1957)

van Geest, William. *God's Earthkeepers: Biblical Action and Reflection on the Environment* (Willowdale, ON: The Evangelical Fellowship of Canada, 1995). Updated in 2007, with 2nd edition available in PDF format (https://files.evangelicalfellowship.ca/si/Environment/God_s_Earthkeepers.pdf).

Vanier, Jean. *Becoming Human (CBC Massey Lecture Series)* (Toronto, ON: House of Anansi Press Inc., 2008).

Volf, Miroslav. *A Public Faith: How Followers of Christ Should Serve the Common Good* (Grand Rapids, MI: Brazos Press, 2011).

Vomiero, Jessica. "As Notre Dame Burned, Parisians Gathered Outside Sang 'Ave Maria'," *Global News*. April 16, 2019 (https://globalnews.ca/news/5172175/notre-dame-crowds-ave-maria).

Wagner, C. Peter. *Acts of the Holy Spirit: A Modern Commentary on the Book of Acts* (Ventura, CA: Regal Books, A Division of Gospel Light, 2000).

Wallace, J. Warner. "A Brief Sample of Archaeology Corroborating the Claims of the New Testament," *Cold-Case Christianity*. June 8, 2018 (http://coldcasechristianity.com/2018/a-brief-sample-of-archaeology-corroborating-the-claims-of-the-new-testament).

Wilberforce, William. *Real Christianity: A Paraphrase in Modern English of a Practical View of the Prevailing Religious System of Professed Christians in the Higher and Middle Classes in This Country, Contrasted with Real Christianity* (Ventura, CA; Regal Books, 2006), 19. Originally published in 1797, revised and updated by Bob Beltz.

Yibeltal, Kalkidan. "Ethiopia 'Breaks' Tree-Planting Record to Tackle Climate Change," *BBC News*. July 29, 2019 (https://www.bbc.com/news/world-africa-49151523).

Yousafzai, Gul, and Asif Shahzad. "Suicide Bombers Attack Church in Pakistan's Quetta Before Christmas, Killing Nine," *Reuters*. December 17, 2017 (https://www.reuters.com/article/us-pakistan-attack/suicide-bombers-attack-church-in-pakistans-quetta-before-christmas-killing-nine-idUSKBN1EB08E).

Movies and Television

100 Huntley Street, "Finding God in the News." Magdalene John. December 1, 2012 (http://www.100huntley.com/watch?id=217815).

Faytene.TV, "Media in Canada, Guest: Lorna Dueck." Faytene Grasseschi. August 4, 2019 (https://www.youtube.com/watch?v=uAGm5nKHvb4&t=1s).

In Search Of..., "The Coming Ice Age." Season 2, Episode 23. Written by Philip Dauber. May 18, 1978.

Inconvenient Truth, An, directed by David Guggenheim (Los Angeles, CA: Paramount Classics, 2006).

Sesame Street. Created by Joan Ganz Cooney and Lloyd Morrisett, produced by Sesame Workshop (previously known as Children's Television Workshop). First episode aired November 10, 1969.

Star Trek, "Bread and Circuses." Season 2, Episode 25. Directed by Ralph Senensky. Written by Gene Roddenberry & Gene L. Coon. NBC, March 15, 1968.

Star Wars, directed by George Lucas (Los Angeles, CA: Twentieth Century Fox, 1977).

Legislative Sources

Constitution Act, 1867, previously, *British North America Act, 1867*, 30 & 31 Victoria, c. 3 (U.K.).

Constitution Act, 1982, Schedule B to the Canada Act 1982, 1982, c. 11 (U.K.).

---. *Canadian Charter of Rights and Freedoms*, Part I of the *Constitution Act, 1982*.

Judicial Sources, with case summary

Alberta v. Hutterian Brethren of Wilson Colony, 2009 SCC 37, [2009] 2 SCR 567.

An Alberta Hutterite colony objected to being photographed, as a violation of the second commandment to not make an image of any likeness on earth. They challenged new security regulations requiring their photos on drivers licenses. The Court concluded this was a minor infringement on religious freedom, and the colony members would have to obtain photo licenses or find other means of transportation.

Caldwell v. Stuart, [1984] 2 SCR 603.

A British Columbia teacher was fired by a Catholic school for violating Catholic practices. The court ruled that the requirement for Catholic school teachers to be practicing Catholics in good standing was legitimate.

Chamberlain v. Surrey School District No. 36, 2002 SCC 86, [2002] 4 SCR 710.

A kindergarten teacher wanted to use children's books about same-sex parents. To avoid controversy with religious parents, the school board refused. The Court sent the decision back to the school board with instruction to reconsider based on tolerance and non-religious assessment, but to include religious parents' concerns as well as the position of other parents in their assessment.

Congrégation des témoins de Jéhovah de St-Jérôme-Lafontaine v. Lafontaine (Village), 2004 SCC 48, [2004] 2 SCR 650.

A Quebec Jehovah's Witness congregation wanted to build a new church building, but municipal officials impeded suitable locations. The Court dealt with the congregation as a single entity, setting guidelines for the village to make an unbiased decision.

Heintz v. Christian Horizons, Ontario Human Rights Tribunal, 2008 HRTO 22 (CanLII), 65 C.C.E.L. (3d) 218, 2063 C.H.R.R. 12, *Ontario Human Rights Commission v. Christian Horizons*, 2010 ONSC 2105.

An employee of a Christian organization contravened conduct expectations by engaging in a same-sex relationship. The Court ruled that each employee's job description would need to indicate a legitimate work-related rationale for the applicability of the organization's statement of faith and lifestyle requirements.

Highwood Congregation of Jehovah's Witnesses (Judicial Committee v. Wall), 2018 SCC 26.

A member of a religious congregation challenged his expulsion for violating membership requirements, partly because of the impact on a business he built based on congregational connections. The Court found no underlying legal right that would allow for judicial review of the congregation's decision, concluding it was not the Court's place to assess or review the beliefs, practices, or proceedings of a private religious organization

Lakeside Colony of Hutterian Brethren v. Hofer, [1992] 3 SCR 165.

Several Hutterites were expelled from their Manitoba colony and refused to leave. The Court concluded the colony could establish membership requirements, but removal had direct economic consequences and required following principles of natural justice.

Loyola High School v. Quebec (Attorney General), 2015 SCC 12, [2015] 1 SCR 613.

A private Catholic school in Montreal objected to being required to teach that all religions are equal. The Court dealt with the school as a school, not just an aggregate of parents, teachers, and students, in making its decision in favour of the school's religious freedom.

Multani v. Commission scolaire Marguerite-Bourgeoys, 2006 SCC 6, [2006] 1 SCR 256.

A Sikh boy's ceremonial knife fell out of his clothes at school and was banned as a weapon. The Court concluded the infringement on religious freedom was significant because the boy was religiously prohibited from being without this symbol of confirmation in his faith.

Parks v. Christian Horizons, Ontario Human Rights Tribunal, 16 CHRR D/40.

Employees of a Christian organization contravened conduct expectations by entering into common-law relationships. The tribunal decided that a religious organization could require statements of faith and lifestyle requirements that defined their expectations as part of the hiring process.

R. v. Big M Drug Mart, [1985] 1 SCR 295.

A Calgary drug store wanted to open on Sundays, in violation of the federal *Lord's Day Act*. The Court concluded the *Act* was unconstitutional because it had a religious purpose.

R. v. Edwards Books, [1986] 2 SCR 713.

Several Toronto stores wanted to open on Sundays, in violation of Ontario's *Retail Business Holidays Act*. The Court concluded the *Act* had a legitimate secular purpose in providing a uniform holiday for retail workers.

R. v. Gruenke, [1991] 3 SCR 263.

A murder was confessed to a church counsellor and the church's pastor. The Court determined that the confidentiality of "religious communications" was to be considered on a case-by-case basis using the four part Wigmore Test:

> (1) The communications must originate in a *confidence* that they will not be disclosed.
>
> (2) This element of *confidentiality must be essential* to the full and satisfactory maintenance of the relation between the parties.
>
> (3) The *relation* must be one which in the opinion of the community ought to be sedulously *fostered*.
>
> (4) The *injury* that would inure to the relation by the disclosure of the communications must be *greater than the benefit* thereby gained for the correct disposal of litigation.

R. v. Oakes, [1986] 1 SCR 103.

The Court set out the test for violation of a *Charter* right to be considered reasonable under section 1. The government initiative violating a right must be:
  i. Prescribed by law
  ii. Have a pressing and substantial purpose
  iii. Be reasonable and demonstrably justified, i.e.
    (a) Rationally connected to the law's purpose, and
    (b) Resulting in minimal impairment of the right
  iv. And, finally, proportionate to attaining the intended effect.

Reference re Same-Sex Marriage, 2004 SCC 79, [2004] 3 SCR 698.

The federal government asked the Court to review draft legislation intended to redefine marriage. The Court ruled that the legislation was within Parliament's jurisdiction, and any change in the definition of marriage would require recognizing the rights of individuals and institutions who hold to a religious definition that might differ from the legislated definition.

Ross v. New Brunswick School District No. 36, [1996] 1 SCR 825.

A parent complained about a teacher who published Holocaust denial and anti-Jewish materials. The Court ruled the school board had a duty to assess activity outside the classroom as part of ensuring that the classroom was a positive place for students.

Saskatchewan (Human Rights Commission) v. Whatcott, 2013 SCC 11, [2013] 1 SCR 467.

A self-described Christian activist was fined by the Human Rights Commission for anti-homosexual flyers he distributed that used Bible quotes. The Court concluded that sacred texts are not hate speech, but how they are used can be.

S.L. v. Commission scolaire des Chênes, 2012 SCC 7, [2012] 1 SCR 235.

Religious parents in Quebec objected to having their children taught that all religions are equal. The Court ruled the challenge premature because the mandatory course about which they were concerned was not yet being taught. The Court commented on the constitutional principle of state neutrality.

Syndicat Northcrest v. Amselem, 2004 SCC 47, [2004] 2 SCR 551.

> Jewish condominium owners wanted to place prayer huts on their balconies for the religious celebration of Sukkot. The Court ruled in their favour, noting that sincerely held religious beliefs, and practices closely connected with those beliefs, are defined by the individuals who hold them.

The Queen v. Jones, [1986] 2 SCR 284.

> An Alberta pastor refused to submit his private home-school-style group to government supervision, as required by law. The Court concluded that parents have a right to determine how their children are educated and the state is entitled to ensure the quality of education.

Trinity Western University v. British Columbia College of Teachers, 2001 SCC 31, [2001] 1 SCR 772.

> The BCCT refused to grant accreditation to TWU's school of education. The Court ruled that once TWU met educational standards, it was to be accredited. The BCCT's regulation of graduates began after they joined the BCCT. The Court concluded the diversity of Canadian society is required to accommodate a diversity of institutions, including religion-based post-secondary education.

Reference

Baxter, J. Sidlow. *Explore The Book: A Basic and Broadly Interpretative Course of Bible Study from Genesis to Revelation (Six Volumes in One)* (Grand Rapids, MI: Zondervan Publishing House, 1979). First published as six volumes in one in 1966.

Bonhoeffer, Dietrich and John W. Doberstein, trans., *Life Together* (New York, NY: HarperCollins Publishers, 1994). Originally published in 1954.

Buckingham, Janet Epp. *Fighting Over God: A Legal and Political History of Religious Freedom in Canada* (Montreal, QC: McGill-Queen's University Press, 2014).

Church, Leslie F., ed. *Commentary on the Whole Bible by Matthew Henry: New One Volume Edition* (Grand Rapids, MI: Zondervan Publishing House, 1980). Originally published in 1960.

Halley, Henry H. *Halley's Bible Handbook*, twenty-fourth edition (Grand Rapids, MI: Zondervan Publishing House, 1996). First edition published in 1924.

Hartill, J. Edwin. *Principles of Biblical Hermeneutics* (Grand Rapids, MI: Zondervan Publishing House, 1997), originally published 1947.

Lewis, Norman, ed. *The New Roget's Thesaurus In Dictionary Form, Revised Edition* (New York, NY: G.P. Putnam's Sons, 1981). Originally published in 1961.

Morehead, Philip D., ed. *The New American Roget's College Thesaurus In Dictionary Form, Revised Edition* (New York, NY: NAL Penguin Inc., 1985).

Newbigin, Lesslie. *Foolishness to the Greeks: The Gospel and Western Culture* (Grand Rapids, MI: Eerdmans, 1988).

Niebuhr, H. Richard. *Christ and Culture (Fiftieth Anniversary Expanded Edition)* (New York, NY: HarperOne, 2001). Originally published in 1951.

Packer, J.I. *Concise Theology: A Guide to Historic Christian Beliefs* (Wheaton, IL: Tyndale House Publishers, Inc., 1993).

Reese, Edward, and Frank Klassen. *The Reese Chronological Bible* (Minneapolis, MN: Bethany House Publishers, 1994). Originally published in 1980.

Stiller, Brian C. *An Insider's Guide to Praying for the World* (Grand Rapids, MI: Bethany House, 2016).

---. *From Jerusalem to Timbuktu: A World Tour of the Spread of Christianity* (Downers Grove, IL: InterVarsity Press, 2018).

---. *From the Tower of Babel to Parliament Hill: How to Be a Christian in Canada Today* (Toronto, ON: HarperCollins Publishers Ltd, 1997).

---. *Jesus and Caesar: Christians in the Public Square* (Oakville, ON: Castle Quay Books Canada, 2003).

Sykes, J.B., ed., *The Concise Oxford Dictionary of Current English, Seventh Edition* (Oxford, U.K.; Oxford University Press, 1982).

Vandezande, Gerald. *Justice, Not Just Us: Faith Perspectives and National Priorities* (Toronto, ON: Public Justice Resource Centre, 1999).

Vine, W.E. and Merrill F. Unger and William White, Jr., eds. *Vine's Complete Expository Dictionary of Old and New Testament Words* (Nashville, TN: Thomas Nelson, Inc., Publishers, 1985).

Walvoord, John F. and Roy B. Zuck, eds. *The Bible Knowledge Commentary: An Exposition of the Scriptures by Dallas Seminary Faculty, New Testament edition* (Wheaton, IL: Victor Books, 1983).

Walvoord, John F. and Roy B. Zuck, eds. *The Bible Knowledge Commentary: An Exposition of the Scriptures by Dallas Seminary Faculty, Old Testament* (Wheaton, IL: Victor Books, 1985).

ABOUT THE AUTHOR

Don Hutchinson, B.A., J.D., studied history and politics at Queen's University, law at the University of British Columbia, and theology with The Salvation Army and at Canada Christian College and School of Graduate Theological Studies. The author of *Under Siege: Religious Freedom and the Church in Canada at 150 (1867–2017)*, Don is recognized as a strategic thinker and planner who is a regular speaker and consultant on religious freedom, strategies for church engagement with culture, and communications in sensitive circumstances.

Following fifteen years in leadership with The Salvation Army, Don consulted with World Vision Canada and others before serving more than seven years on The Evangelical Fellowship of Canada's leadership team as Vice-President, General Legal Counsel, and Director of the EFC's Centre for Faith and Public Life. He then acted as interim National Director/CEO for Canadian Bible Society while CBS conducted a CEO search.

A member of the Law Society of Ontario, Don has appeared before the Supreme Court of Canada on several occasions as well as a number of parliamentary committees. In addition to being featured in print, as well as on television, radio, and online media, this avid motorcyclist has served on the boards of local and national charities.

Don was honoured with the Queen Elizabeth II Diamond Jubilee medal for contributions to Canadian Society. Don and Gloria have been married more than thirty-five years. They have a daughter and a grandson.

CHURCH IN SOCIETY

Don currently serves as Principal of *Ansero Services*, a Christian ministry focused on facilitating partnerships for Christians engaged on issues of religious freedom in Canada and internationally.

Find more at:
www.donhutchinson.ca

Also by the Author

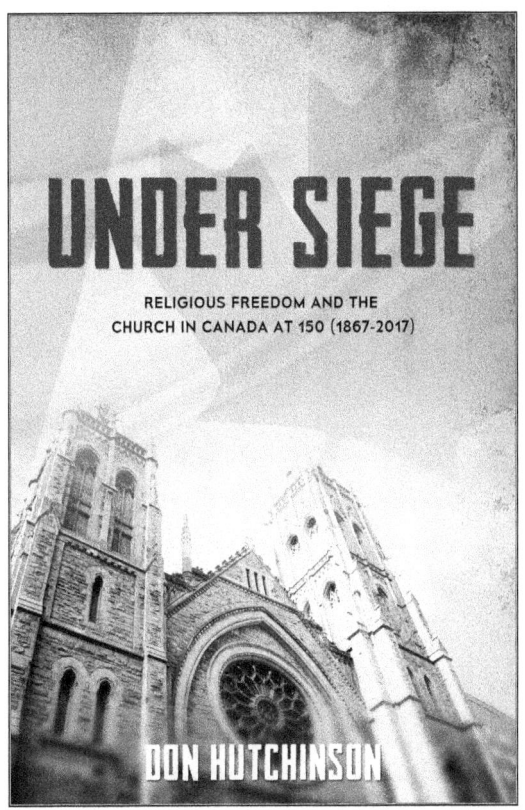

Writing from the perspective of a student of life, history, law, politics, and theology, Don Hutchinson draws on all of these areas in *Under Siege* to offer perceptive insight into the Christian Church of today's Canada. The reader will receive the benefit of his thirty years of church leadership, Christian witness, constitutional law, and public policy experience to gain a practical understanding of how we, the Church, may cast the deciding votes on the future of Christianity in our constitutionally guaranteed "free and democratic society."

www.ingramcontent.com/pod-product-compliance
Lightning Source LLC
Chambersburg PA
CBHW070610170426
43200CB00012B/2648